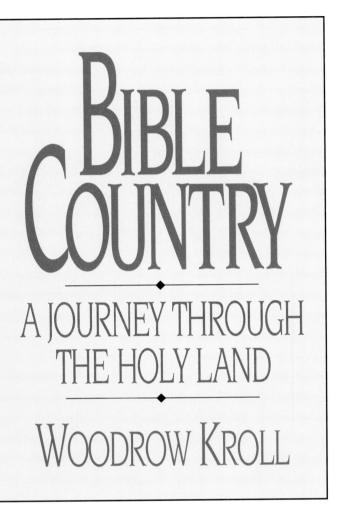

BIBLE COUNTRY

A JOURNEY THROUGH THE HOLY LAND

WOODROW KROLL

Printed in the United States of America

10,000 printed to date—1992
(5-7968—10M—32)
ISBN 0-8474-1455-8

Cover and interior design
Joe Ragont Studios, Inc.

Edited by Beth C. Nilson

Unless otherwise noted, all Scripture quotations are from
The New King James Version.

TO MY CHILDREN,
TRACY, TIM, TINA AND TIFFANY

PREFACE

I was 19 at the time. It was my first trip abroad. Six others and I shipped our car to Belgium, and from there we drove across Europe, through Greece and Turkey, even through Syria and Lebanon, on our way to the Holy Land. Then we turned around and drove back throughout Europe and the British Isles. It was too good to be true—the adventure of a lifetime.

You would expect that after I had visited Paris, London, Zurich, Rome and Athens the same summer, one of these great cities would dominate my memory. But even repeated visits to each of these cities have not made the impression on me that one city has. What city has more style than the stylish capitals of Europe? What city dwarfs all others in importance? What is the most unforgettable city on earth? There's no question about it—JERUSALEM.

Most Christians dream of visiting the Holy Land. Someone said that ten days in the Holy Land is equal to a semester in seminary, but for one who has spent many years in seminaries and made dozens of trips to the Holy Land, I'd say that is an understatement. The most practical understanding of Bible archaeology, history and geography came to me from actually being there, in Bible Country. I can describe things to you in word pictures, but the only real way for you to absorb the land of the Bible is to see it firsthand.

Bible Country is designed to be of benefit both to the traveler and the dreamer. That's important, because dreamers somehow have the habit of becoming travelers. This is an armchair guide to the Holy Land. As you sit before your fireplace in an easy chair, your feet stretched out before you, this guide will transport you in mind and spirit to the hills of Galilee and the mountains of Judaea. You will live the Holy Land experience as best you can without actually being there. But when that exciting day comes and your jumbo jet lands in the Promised Land—and it surely will—you won't want to leave this book behind. It will then be an invaluable guide to you as you sit in an air-conditioned coach on a plush seat, your feet stretched out before you.

Special thanks to three friends who have assisted me in the writing of *Bible Country*. I am indebted to Cathy Strate, herself a Holy Land traveler, who typed and retyped the manuscript, and to an Arab friend, Abed Hawash, and a Jewish friend, Malcolm Cartier, both residents of Jerusalem, who substantiated the accuracy of the statistical data in the book.

There is simply no place on earth like the Holy Land. It never loses its luster. After I had been to Jerusalem at least a dozen times before, I arrived after dark one night champing at the bit to get to the Old City. I couldn't sleep at all that night because of my excitement! Jerusalem the golden, the city of God. It's unlike any other city in the world, as the Holy Land is unlike any other place in the world.

Although we have highlighted the places of most interest to Christians, nonetheless this guide to the Holy Land will be of real value to all. It is my prayer that *Bible Country* will not just bring you to a greater appreciation of the land of the Lord but to the Lord of the land as well. May it contribute to the holy life of all who read it, and may your Holy Land experience be an exciting one.

Woodrow Kroll

Lincoln, Nebraska

CONTENTS

CHAPTER ONE

BIBLE COUNTRY– ITS WELCOME

"And thus you shall say to him who lives in prosperity:peace be to you, peace to your house, and peace to all that you have!"

1 Samuel 25:6

SHALOM! SALAAM! HELLO! When you arrive in Israel, you'll hear all three of these greetings—in Hebrew, Arabic and English. This is your welcome to one of the oldest nations on earth, yet one of the newest.

Disembark, and you'll discover a land of incredible contrasts. Here lie the ruins of the world's ancient civilizations—the Phoenician, Philistine, Hebrew, Nabatean, Roman and Greek. Yet amid these ruins rise the skyscrapers of Tel Aviv, Jerusalem and Haifa. The land abounds with artifacts, excavations and amateur archaeologists. Yet today it blossoms like a rose.

Here you'll be taken back to the days of Jesus as if in some mysterious time machine. For as you walk the shadowy streets of Old Jerusalem, you'll see the blind, the beggar, the destitute. You'll be jostled about by the crowd and brushed by the overladen donkey being led to the marketplace. As you stroll over the hills of Samaria, you'll climb a knoll which was taken in battle by Joshua, and again by David, and again by Judas Maccabaeus, and again by Moshe Dayan.

In this land, as in no other, you can relive Bible history, retrace Bible geography and recapture Bible familiarity. In Israel you don't just read about the past; you experience it. You are in Bible Country, the Promised Land, the Holy Land.

CHAPTER TWO

BIBLE COUNTRY— ITS PEOPLE

"If the Lord delights in us, then He will bring us into this land and give it to us, 'a land which flows with milk and honey.' Only do not rebel against the Lord, nor fear the people of the land, for they are our bread; their protection has departed from them, and the Lord is with us. Do not fear them."

Numbers 14:8,9

When the 12 spies were sent on a reconnaissance mission to spy out the Promised Land, they reported, "The Amalekites dwell in the land of the South; the Hittites, the Jebusites, and the Amorites dwell in the mountains; and the Canaanites dwell by the sea and along the banks of the Jordan" (Numbers 13:29).

The people in Israel today—nearly five million of them—are as diverse as the people in Moses' day. Here are some Israelis you will meet, grouped according to religion. (Is there any other way to classify people in the Holy Land?)

THE JEWS

In general the Jews of Israel are rough, outgoing and brash—almost to the point of arrogance. But don't let that rough exterior fool you. Once you get to know them, you come to love them. About half are immigrants; the other half, born in Israel, are called

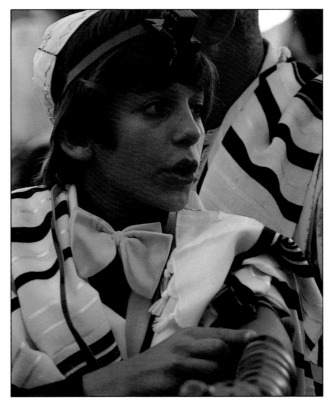

A young Sabra at his bar mitzvah

"Sabras." (The Sabra is an indigenous fruit of the cactus family which is prickly on the outside but sweet on the inside.) About 15 different Jewish sects are represented in the nearly four million Jews.

THE SAMARITANS

There are only about 500 Samaritans remaining. They are of mixed ancestry and were barred by the Jews from rebuilding Jerusalem after the Babylonian Exile (cf. Ezra 4:1-3; Nehemiah 4:1-8). They recognize only the Pentateuch, the five books of Moses, as God's Word; and they maintain a synagogue on Mount Gerizim, which they hold to be the sacred mountain of God. Most of them live in Nablus, the capital of the Arab West Bank.

THE KARAITES

The Karaites number a little more than 10,000 and live chiefly in Ramla. They repudiate the oral traditions of the rabbis and expound only the Old Testament. This Jewish sect was founded in Baghdad in A.D. 706 by Anan ben David.

THE MUSLIMS

Muslims are followers of the seventh-century A.D. prophet Mohammed and the religion of Islam. They believe that there is but one God, Allah, and that Mohammed was his prophet. Almost all of them are Arabs, and they number approximately 663,400. There are more than 800 mosques in Israel, and the number is increasing. Since the Six Day War they live in the occupied territory of the West Bank, the Gaza Strip and East Jerusalem.

THE DRUZES

These Arabic-speaking people believe that there is but one God who has revealed Himself in successive incarnations—the final and most perfect incarnation being that of Al-Hakim, the sixth Fatimid Caliph of Egypt (A.D. 996-1021). They follow the Bible and venerate men from its pages, especially Jethro, father-in-law of Moses. Because of intermarriage with the Romans and Crusaders, many of the Druzes are blond, with large swarthy mustaches. Generally they live on the Golan Heights. Several Druzes serve in the Knesset, Israel's Parliament.

THE BAHA'IS

Bahaism is an eclectic religion that emphasizes the unity of mankind and the commonality of all religions. The forerunner of the movement, Mirza Ali Mohammed, a descendant of the prophet Mohammed, was born and martyred in Iran during the last century. One of his followers, Mirza Husayn Ali,

The face of this modern-day sheik brings to mind images of Abraham and the patriarchs.

was also born in Iran but died in the Holy Land after a 24-year imprisonment in Acre. Most of the Baha'i doctrines came from him. The world center of the faith is located on the side of Mount Carmel at Haifa.

THE CHRISTIANS

You may be surprised to learn that about 106,000 Christians live in Israel. Most of them are Arabs and fall into four main categories: (1) Protestant (Anglican, Baptist, Lutheran); (2) Catholic (Roman, Greek, Armenian); (3) Orthodox (Greek, Romanian, Russian); and (4) Monophysite (Armenian, Coptic, Ethiopian). Many Christian sites are maintained in the Holy Land, and spending Christmas in Bethlehem is a lifelong dream of many of the faithful.

THE BEDOUIN

Although not a religious sect, the Bedouin comprise a group worth noting. Their total population in Israel is 110,000, but 60 percent now live in permanent settlements instead of residing in the familiar black-tented camps. Those who remain seminomadic usually do

Always the perfect host, this Bedouin brews a glass of tea for every visitor to his tent.

The marketplace, called the "souk" in Arabic, is always a center of activity.

not respect traditional land boundaries but take their flocks to graze wherever they find grass. They produce one of the most incongruous sights in the modern Holy Land —television antennas over Bedouin tents that scan the Palestine skies in search of American TV reruns.

WHERE PEOPLE LIVE

While the Bedouin move from hillside to valley and back again, most Israelis (86.25 percent) have settled in the 114 towns and cities of the land. Today thousands of people live in cities inhabited by their ancestors in Old and New Testament times. Those Is-

A SLICE FROM THE ECONOMY

With a soaring annual inflation rate and sporadic heightened tensions, the haggling shopkeepers of Old Jerusalem seemingly lead a hand-to-mouth existence. Still, at night many of them slide into the family Mercedes, exuberant over the day's profits.

COMMUNICATION

The official language of Israel is Hebrew (a tongue which all but disappeared through disuse until the establishment of the state of Israel). However, Arabic, Yiddish, English, French, German, Polish and Russian are also commonly spoken, and all road signs are given in Hebrew, Arabic and English.

EATING IN THE HOLY LAND

Israelis are hearty eaters. Breakfast is likely to be the most elaborate meal of the day. A typical breakfast consists of a buffet of fresh fruits, cheeses, juices, boiled eggs, herring, sardines and other delicacies. Breakfast also includes cucumbers, radishes, onions, tomatoes and a wide variety of raw and luscious vegetables. As you experience an Israeli breakfast you may hear a faint voice echo, "We remember the fish which we ate freely in Egypt, the cucumbers, the melons, the leeks, the onions, and the garlic" (Numbers 11:5).

Israel's modern answer to ancient manna is pita. It is a flat, pancake-shaped Arab bread, usually six inches in diameter and split in the middle. When pita bread is stuffed with salad and balls of deep-fried ground chick peas and spiced with peppers and other oriental delights, the result is an unforgettable delight known as felafel. No one can truthfully say he has imbibed the spirit of the Holy Land until he has sampled a felafel from an eager vendor on the streets of Old Jerusalem.

If you eat all this with humus, a paste made from ground chick peas and olive oil, or tchina, a similar paste made from ground sesame seeds, you will not soon forget either the experience or the flavor. Perhaps this food contributes to the temperament of the Middle East.

raelis who do not live in urban centers tend to live in one of two kinds of settlements—the kibbutz or the moshav.

The kibbutz is a village in which property is commonly owned by the members. Those who choose to join a kibbutz have all their needs satisfied by the community. Nearly everything is communal—the dining room, classroom, cultural and sports centers and clinic. Married couples occupy small apartments, but children are cared for in a nursery or kindergarten. Kibbutzim are largely agri-cultural in nature, and most invite guests to visit their villages. Today in Israel there are 270 kibbutzim with a membership of 124,900.

The moshav is a family-owned, cooperative village. The farmsteads are individually owned; but they have a unique system of mutual aid, collective development and cooperative purchasing and marketing. Most of the machinery is owned and operated by the moshavim rather than by individual farmers. Today Israel boasts 454 moshavim with a population of 158,500.

CHAPTER THREE

BIBLE COUNTRY– THE LAND

"For the LORD your God is bringing you into a good land, a land of brooks of water, of fountains and springs, that flow out of valleys and hills; a land of wheat and barley, of vines and fig trees and pomegranates; a land of olive oil and honey; a land in which you will eat bread without scarcity, in which you will lack nothing; a land whose stones are iron and out of whose hills you can dig copper."

Deuteronomy 8:7-9

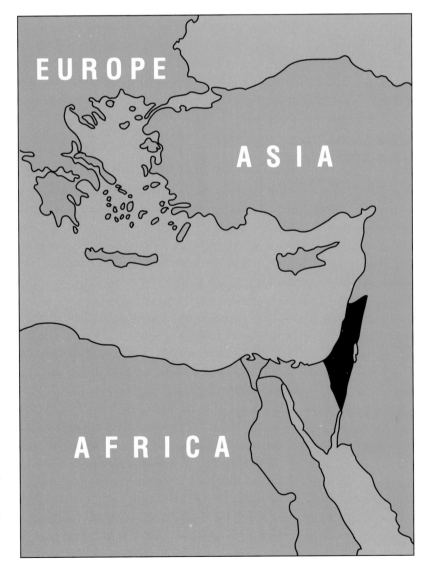

Just look at a map and you'll understand why the war-ravaged land of Israel is so important. God cast it geographically as the land-bridge between three major continents. It acts as a hinge between Europe and Asia, with Africa hanging by a small thread at the Suez Canal. The armies of history have marched through this land on their way to victory or defeat.

In this jet age the country may seem small. The distance from "Dan to Beersheba" is only 150 miles, and the entire state of Israel is just a bit larger than Connecticut.

Nevertheless, Israel's terrain is incredibly diverse. Mountains, deserts, lowlands, plateaus, rivers, lakes, fresh and saltwater seas—all are found within its borders. When you examine the five natural regions of the land, you will see that Palestine's orientation is vertical.

MAJOR REGIONS

Whether you dock at the port of Haifa or land at Ben-Gurion Airport in Lod, your first steps in the Promised Land are on the COASTAL PLAIN. This narrow strip of land begins at the base of Mount Carmel, where the plain is only a few hundred feet wide. It continues south through the luxuriant Plain of Sharon to the gently rolling hills of Philistia, and then it vanishes into the desert south of Gaza. Nearly two-thirds of modern Israel's population lives along this Mediterranean plain in cities such as Haifa, Tel Aviv/Jaffa, Ashdod and Ashkelon.

The second natural region is the CENTRAL HIGHLANDS, sometimes called the Western Hills. Rising more than 6000 feet in Lebanon, this mountain range averages between 2000 and 3000 feet in Israel. This monotonous mass of mountains encompasses the areas referred to in biblical times as Upper and Lower Galilee, the Hill Country of Ephraim and the Hill Coun-

try of Judah. Safed, Nablus, Jerusalem and Bethlehem are all located in these mountains.

In striking contrast to the highlands is the JORDAN VALLEY, known as the Rift Valley. This deep depression begins between the Lebanon and Anti-Lebanon Mountains and continues south through the Sea of Galilee. It follows the course of the Jordan River to the Dead Sea and then continues southward

to the Gulf of Aqabah and the Red Sea. Running between two great geological faults, this area contains the lowest spot on earth—the Dead Sea—Jericho, Beth Shean and the cities that dot the shores of the Sea of Galilee.

Again the terrain of Palestine changes abruptly as the Jordan Valley rises on the east to the TRANSJORDAN PLATEAU. Generally belonging to the Hashemite Kingdom of Jordan, these eastern hills tower over the Great Rift as the western hills do on the opposite side.

The final natural region of the Holy Land is the NEGEV. Situated south of Palestine, this steppe is like an inverted pyramid that provides the base for the "sculpture" we have come to know affectionately as the Holy Land. The Negev contains more than 12,500 square miles of sand and barrenness. The only inhabitable area is a small strip about 30 miles wide around Beersheba.

Mountains of the Negev

PLANTS, ANIMALS AND MINERALS

Bounded by her Arab neighbors, Lebanon on the north, Syria on the northeast, Jordan on the east and Egypt on the southwest, Israel is the most agricultural country in the Middle East today. More than 1,083,250 cultivated areas blanket the Israeli hills and plains. Much of the blossoming of modern Israel is due to irrigation. In fact, 67 percent of Israel's water supply is used for agriculture.

Because of the subtropical climate and the ingenious use of water, Israel's flora is among the richest in the world, with 3000 species of plants. By comparison, Great Britain has only 1700 species. Tree planting in Israel has almost become a ritual. Although the land was heavily wooded in Bible times, centuries of warfare destroyed the forests. Since 1948 a total of 190 million trees have been planted on 300,000 acres of the Promised Land by both natives and pilgrims.

Like her flora, Israel's fauna abounds with species from all over the world. These include the leopard, hyena, jackal, porcupine, antelope, wild boar, wolf, coney, ibex and many more. Four hundred species of birds also are found; and as in the days of the Old Testament, eagles, ospreys and vultures nest in the crags of the highest mountains.

And just as God promised in Deuteronomy 8:9, the Holy Land abounds in mineral wealth. Mineral deposits in commercial quantity include bromide, potash, copper, phosphates, clay, sulphur, bitumen and manganese. Is it any wonder that God calls this a "good land"?

CLIMATE

In the Holy Land you can frolic in the subtropical heat of Eilat and ski the slopes of Mount Hermon in the same season.

Although the land lies at about the same latitude as Georgia or Southern California, much of her climate is determined by the configuration of her mountains and her proximity to the desert.

The Israeli seasons are but two—winter and summer. Israeli winters start with the "early" rains. These rains, which begin in October and get heavier over the next three months, mark the beginning of the major agricultural season. Sometimes these rains turn to snow in Jerusalem and other higher elevations. The "latter" rains arrive in March and continue for a month or more until the crop is ripened (Jeremiah 3:3; Amos 4:7). It almost never rains between May and September.

As in David's day, the land drinks water by the rain from heaven (Deuteronomy 11:11). Average rainfall at Acco on the coastal plain is about 25 inches. Jerusalem averages 19 inches annually and Beersheba, 8 inches. The lower Jordan Valley receives only one or two inches of rainfall per year.

Holy Land temperatures are moderate. January and July averages for major cities are:

City	January	July
Jerusalem	45-57	67-83
Tel Aviv	48-66	71-87
Tiberias	54-69	77-98
Eilat	52-72	80-105

But be aware that the combination of oppressive humidity and the brilliant sun make the summer days of Jericho and other cities of the Jordan Valley almost unbearable.

CHAPTER FOUR

BIBLE COUNTRY
—ITS HISTORY

*"And the Lord said to Abram . . . 'Lift your eyes now and look from
the place where you are—northward, southward, eastward, and westward;
for all the land which you see I give to you and your descendants forever.'"*

Genesis 13:14,15

Neither the buzzing of Israeli jets overhead nor the cosmopolitan nature of the population can diminish the fact that this is an ancient land. It exudes history. It provides a constant reminder of God's promises to His people. It is "a land for which the LORD your God cares; the eyes of the LORD your God are always on it, from the beginning of the year to the very end of the year" (Deuteronomy 11:12). Of all the terrestrial acreage created by God, this land alone, old and new, is the Holy Land.

But the history of this troubled land reads like the rough draft of *War and Peace*, with the accent on war. Since the day the LORD God promised the land to Israel, invaders from far and near have trampled the grain of Israel's fields.

In nearly 4000 years of occupation this land has produced the three great religions of the world but has failed to produce a lasting peace. In 4000 years the Promised Land has come full circle and is again occupied by the descendants of Abraham. The Babylonians, Persians, Greeks, Romans, Egyptians, Turks and others notwithstanding, the promise of God to Abraham in Genesis 13 is as sure today as it was the day the patriarch left Ur in search of a homeland.

The outline overview of Israel's history on the next two pages graphically displays her checkered dominance.

CONQUERORS OF CANAAN

THE JEWS (1900–587 B.C.)

1900 B.C.   Abraham the patriarch entered Palestine, then known as Canaan, for it was controlled by Amorites and Canaanites.

1630 B.C.   Jacob moved patriarchal family to Egypt to be with Joseph.

1250 B.C.   Joshua and the Israelites reentered the land of Canaan. Some date this event to 1400 B.C.

1200 B.C.   Philistines invaded the land from Crete.

1025 B.C.   Saul was crowned Israel's first king.

1004 B.C.   David ascended to the throne of Israel.

965 B.C.   Solomon succeeded David as Israel's king.

920 B.C.   Israel was divided into Northern and Southern tribes.

721 B.C.   Assyrians captured Samaria, capital of Northern tribes. Captives were taken, and they vanished into the pages of history.

THE BABYLONIANS (587–539 B.C.)

587 B.C.   Nebuchadnezzar, king of Babylon, sacked Jerusalem, capital of the Southern tribes, and took Judah captive.

THE PERSIANS (539–334 B.C.)

539 B.C.   Cyrus, king who conquered Babylonia, decreed that Jewish captives might return to homeland. Reparation began.

516 B.C.   Second temple at Jerusalem rebuilt.

458 B.C.   Ezra instituted reforms and God instituted revival in Jerusalem.

444 B.C.   Nehemiah led a company of workers to rebuild Jerusalem's wall. The work was accomplished in 52 days.

THE GREEKS (334–167 B.C.)

334 B.C.   Alexander the Great vanquished Palestine. After his death Ptolemies and Seleucids ruled the land.

175 B.C.   The Seleucid king, Antiochus IV Epiphanes, desecrated the temple altar by offering a pig on it.

THE HASMONEANS (167–63 B.C.)

167 B.C.   Aged priest Mattathias and his sons revolted against the Seleucids. The Maccabees gave nearly a century of peace to Palestine.

THE ROMANS (63 B.C.–A.D. 330)

63 B.C.   Roman general Pompey conquered Palestine.

39 B.C.   Herod the Great expelled the Parthians, reigned until 4 B.C. Jesus Christ was born during his reign.

A.D. 30   This was the approximate date of Christ's crucifixion.

A.D. 66   Jewish zealots revolted against Roman rule.

A.D. 70   Jerusalem was sacked and burned by the Roman general Titus.

A.D. 73   Masada, last zealot stronghold, fell to the Romans.

A.D. 132   Under Bar Kokhba the Jews revolted a second time unsuccessfully.

THE BYZANTINES (A.D. 313–634)

A.D. 313   Constantine issued the Edict of Milan, bringing freedom of worship to all religions. Constantinople (Byzantium) was made capital of eastern half of Roman Empire.

A.D. 614   Persians retook Palestine, and 33,877 people were slain. Christian churches were destroyed.

OVER THE CENTURIES

THE ARABS (A.D. 634–1099)

A.D. 632   The prophet Mohammed, who was born in Mecca in 570, died, but his religion spread over the Arab world.

A.D. 1009   Al-Hakim, the mad Fatimid Caliph, began persecution of Christians and Jews in the Holy Land. The Church of the Holy Sepulchre was among the 30,000 Christian buildings destroyed.

THE CRUSADERS (A.D. 1099–1291)

A.D. 1099   Jerusalem was captured by the Crusaders.

A.D. 1187   Saladin routed the Christian Crusaders at the Horns of Hattin in Galilee. Thus, the Christian influence was gone from Palestine.

A.D. 1263   Mameluke Sultan Baybars of Egypt continued to capture remaining Crusader strongholds.

THE MAMELUKES (A.D. 1291–15__

THE JEWS (A.D. 1917—)

A.D. 1917   The Balfour Declaration recognized the historic connection between the Jewish people and Palestine. It pledged support for a national home for the Jews.

A.D. 1947   The United Nations partitioned Palestine between Israel and Jordan.

A.D. 1948   On May 14 the State of Israel was established. The British withdrew; the Israeli-Arab war began. War ended July 18.

A.D. 1956   Egypt nationalized the Suez Canal. On July 26, 1956, Israel attacked and occupied nearly all the Sinai but later withdrew to 1949 armistice lines.

A.D. 1967   Egyptian president Nasser closed the Gulf of Aqabah to Israeli shipping. The Six Day War, a blitzkrieg attack by Israeli air and ground units, resulted in

CHAPTER FIVE

SAND DUNES AND SCENIC DELIGHTS

THE COASTAL PLAIN

"Then the LORD spoke to Moses, saying, 'Command the children of Israel, and say to them: "When you come into the land of Canaan, this is the land that shall fall to you as an inheritance—the land of Canaan to its boundaries. . . . As for the western border, you shall have the Great Sea for a border."'"

Numbers 34:1,2,6

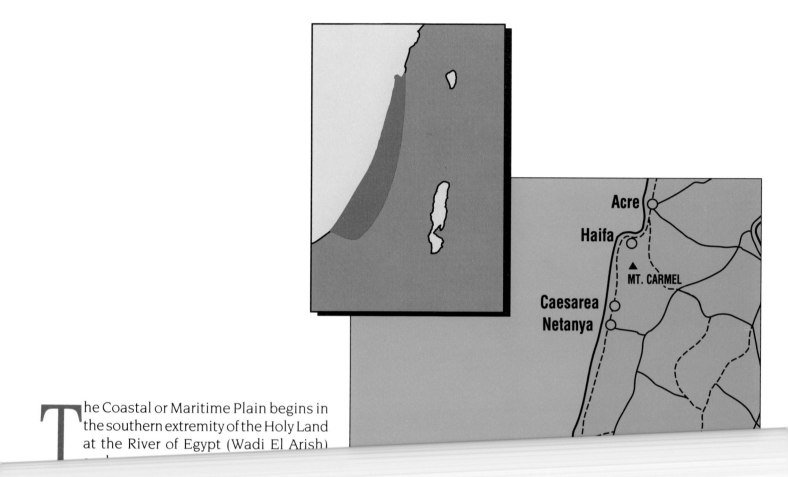

Acre
Haifa
▲
MT. CARMEL
Caesarea
Netanya

T he Coastal or Maritime Plain begins in
the southern extremity of the Holy Land
at the River of Egypt (Wadi El Arish)

Above: View of Tel Aviv from Jaffa

Below: Simon the Tanner's house in Jaffa

THE ROAD NORTH

TEL AVIV

The largest all-Jewish community in the world, TEL AVIV is a model product of the twentieth century. It is noisy, frantic, crowded, uncoordinated, cosmopolitan and delightful. It is a microcosm of all of Israel. This rapidly growing metropolis is the business, entertainment and cultural center of Israel.

A striking feature of this modern city's skyline is the sparkling white Shalom Tower (Migdal Shalom). The glass-elevator ride to the observatory, up 34 stories to the top, gives a grand view of the city and the Coastal Plain in general. From this vantage point the main streets of Tel Aviv look like squiggly strands of spaghetti laid parallel to the coastline.

Like any modern metropolis, Tel Aviv has its share of museums, theaters and parks, including the handsome campus of Tel Aviv University. This is the largest university in Israel, with nearly 20,000 students. The Tel Aviv Zoo, at the end of Ben-Gurion Boulevard, specializes in near-extinct animals. At the zoo you can see Aldabras tortoises, Swinhoe pheasants, Cyprus wild sheep and Syrian bears, among a host of other species.

Tel Aviv is a city born of necessity. In 1909, tired of cramped quarters in the Jewish sector of the Arab city of Jaffa, 60 families bought 32 acres of sand dunes on Jaffa's northern outskirts and planted their own town. Led by Meir Dizengoff, these 250 people named their settlement Tel Aviv ("Hill of Spring," Ezekiel 3:15). Dizengoff prophesied that one day their small town would contain as many as 25,000 residents. His estimate was grossly inadequate.

During World War I the Turkish general dispossessed the Tel Avivians, but they returned when General Allenby's British Army ousted the Turks and the war ended. The city's motto, "I shall build thee and thou shalt be built," has inspired many immigrating Jews to remain right in Tel Aviv rather than to brave the sands of the Negev or the mortar shells of northern Galilee.

Tel Aviv also has an ancient history. From 1955 to 1961, an archaeologist named Kaplan discovered artifacts above the harbor which date back to the eighteenth century B.C. Here, too, a Hyksos citadel was discovered, with walls 20 feet thick and a city gate inscribed with the name Ramses II, who lived during the thirteenth century B.C. The city of Israel's future is built on the cities of Israel's past.

JAFFA (JOPPA)

Interlocked with Tel Aviv, one of the world's newest cities, is JAFFA, one of the world's oldest cities. Greater Tel Aviv/Jaffa is now a sprawling complex with a population of

350,000, but Jaffa's history dates to biblical days.

These two cities are like two candles placed so close together that their flames flicker as one. Whereas Jaffa was the original city, Tel Aviv became her unwanted offspring. Now the old section of Jaffa is but an oriental balcony overlooking the mushrooming metropolis.

There is one spot you must visit in Jaffa. Wind your way up the climbing streets of Old Jaffa. High on the hill above the harbor you will find the Franciscan Monastery of Saint Peter. Close to it, in a narrow alley, you will discover a mosque built in 1730, the oldest in Jaffa. According to Christian tradition, this is where the house of Simon the tanner stood (Acts 10:5,6,32), where Peter had the vision of the great sheet.

Get your camera ready to photograph one of the quaintest scenes in the Holy Land. Face the harbor below and shoot a picture of the mosque, using the blue-green waters of the Mediterranean as a backdrop.

NETANYA

When you leave the glamor and glitter of Tel Aviv behind, take the coastal road on the

JAFFA: A CITY WITH A HISTORY

The harbor of Jaffa is one of the oldest in the world. Known as Japho in Joshua's time (Joshua 19:46), it became the chief seaport of ancient Israel. Here the famous cedars of Lebanon were brought en route to Jerusalem and Solomon's Temple (II Chronicles 2:16; Ezra 3:7). Joppa was the seaport city where Jonah embarked to go to Tarshish in his futile attempt to run from God (Jonah 1:3).

This was the home of Tabitha, or Dorcas, who was raised from the dead by Peter (Acts 9:36-43). Here Peter learned, through a vision of a great sheet, that God was as interested in the salvation of the Gentiles as He was in the salvation of the Jews (Acts 9:43—10:48).

Many others, including Richard the Lion-Hearted and Napoleon, have come by way of Jaffa. The ancient harbor and Crusader fortifications are but a few of the reminders of a former glory now swallowed up in urban living.

ishing trade. (Shades of the splendor of

More than 2000 overseas members have joined the club, but nonmembers may play the course as well.

Just beyond the course you can see the clear outline of a Roman hippodrome. More than 1000 feet long and built to accommodate 20,000 spectators, this hippodrome was once the site of enthusiastic crowds watching spirited horse races. Today it is but a grassy rectangular depression in the ground. Beyond the hippodrome you will notice, if you look closely, a number of second- and third-century statues of Roman emperors.

The two major sites of Caesarea are dead ahead. First, there is the port of Herod and the Crusader fortress of St. Louis. Enter the city from the side by the sea. Climb the steps on the right to the top of the mound that overlooks everything. As you face the Mediterranean, you can actually see the outlines of Herod's great harbor.

Herod the Great had a penchant for building. One look at Jerusalem, Samaria, Masada and other cities in the Holy Land will convince you of that. Since the Palestinian coast is smooth and quite regular, it did not provide a good harbor. Herod determined to build an artificial harbor at Caesarea and make it the chief seaport. The Jewish historian Josephus records that the king succeeded very well (Antiq. XV.9.6; Wars I,23).

The man-made harbor consisted of a semi-circular sea wall, or barrier, 50 feet long and 18 feet wide, built in water 30 fathoms deep. This semicircle opened toward the sea. Originally each end of this barrier was dominated by a tower. Ships would pass through the seaward opening and into the harbor to unload their cargo. It is estimated that some of the stones used in the sea wall were 50 feet long. As you peer into the blue waters below, you can clearly see the outlines of the harbor.

Before you leave the mound, take a panoramic view and drink in the beauty of the fertile valley, eerie sand dunes, magnificent ruins and a sea of unmatched beauty. Breathe in that salt air and behold the pageant of God's goodness. Watch the breakers crash into the sea wall and billow up like puffy clouds. What a sight! Then retrace your steps to the city below and make your way to the Crusader fortress gate.

Originally the fortress was about one-tenth the size of the city itself, and it comprised some 30 acres. The main gate, which consists of a Gothic gate tower and an adjacent vaulted street, has been restored.

As you walk along the walls of the city, you will notice that the granite columns were laid horizontally throughout the walls. The Crusaders did this to keep the walls from being undermined from without. In the hall of the main gate you can see the slit windows from which Crusader archers could shoot their

Roman aqueduct at Caesarea

CAESAREA—RICH IN BIBLICAL HISTORY

As you stand in the midst of the dusty debris that was once Caesarea, the sailors' paradise, shut your eyes.

You are in the city that was once the home of the Roman procurators, including Pontius Pilate. Here Herod Agrippa died, being "eaten by worms" (Acts 12:19-23), because he denied God the glory due Him.

Caesarea was the home of Cornelius, the centurion who believed and was baptized when Peter preached to him (Acts 10). After Peter was delivered from prison (Acts 12:19), he visited this city a second time.

Philip the evangelist and his four daughters lived here (Acts 8:40). According to Acts 21:8,9, his daughters prophesied here. While Paul was in Caesarea, Agabus prophesied that Paul would be imprisoned in Jerusalem (Acts 21:10-13). And after being taken into custody, the apostle was escorted back to Caesarea by a group of soldiers (Acts 23:23-33).

Open your eyes and look at what some say is Paul's Caesarean prison. Nearby, Paul made three outstanding defenses of Christianity—first, before Felix, the governor of Judaea (Acts 24:1-22); two years later before Festus, who succeeded Felix (Acts 25:1-12); and finally before King Agrippa (Acts 26).

Several years later, the Roman massacre of Jews in Caesarea precipitated the great revolt of A.D. 66. This was crushed when Jerusalem was destroyed by the Romans in A.D. 70.

By the end of the first century A.D. the city had a healthy Christian community. In the third century A.D. the Christian scholar Origen founded the School of Caesarea. The great church historian Eusebius was bishop of Caesarea from A.D. 313 to 340. The Crusader fortifications were built by Louis XIV of France in A.D. 1251.

Stone with inscription bearing the name of Pontius Pilate

most significant archaeological discoveries of Caesarea. If you're familiar with Latin, you'll know that the inscription bears the names of Emperor Tiberias and Pontius Pilate. Pilate, you'll recall, ruled Judaea as Roman procurator between A.D. 26 and 36 and was the government official who could find no fault with Jesus Christ (Matthew 27:24) but scourged Him nonetheless (John 19:1). This is the only known inscription bearing Pilate's name. It confirms the description of the man given in the New Testament and by Josephus, the first century A.D. Jewish historian. Although the real stone is now in the Israel National Museum, this duplicate is worthy of a picture.

Ancient Tragedy

The amphitheater is reminiscent of a miniature Roman Coliseum. Enter through the back and near the top. This ancient structure has obviously been restored. The numbered seats give evidence of summer theatrical and musical performances during the annual Israel Festival. (The first performance in the 100-yard-long, 60-yard-wide amphitheater in more than 1700 years came in the summer of 1961, when Pablo Casals played.)

This site breathes of ancient tragedy. Almost certainly gladiators fought with lions here to entertain the Roman citizens. Here Vespasian was hailed as emperor by his soldiers. Here, too, Titus celebrated the birthday of his brother Domitian by pitting the beasts of the amphitheater against 2500 Jews in a classic act of Roman butchery. If the stones and columns you see strewn between the amphitheater and the beach could talk, you'd hear a tale of horror.

It is ironic, isn't it, that a city of so much culture and grace could exhibit so much cruelty and debauchery in the name of entertainment. The ruins of this ancient Caesarean amphitheater stand as mute yet mighty testimony of man's innate unacceptability to God. Ancient Rome's period of power was similar to Noah's day when "the LORD saw that the wickedness of man was great in the earth, and that every intent of the thoughts

arrows. Leave the urban area of ancient Caesarea by way of the bridge over the once impressive moat that encircled the city. Today this moat is but a bed for the abundant vegetation that grows from its unused walls.

If you travel to the south side of the city, you can visit the second major site of Caesarea—the magnificent Roman amphitheater. Here the splendor of ancient Rome is graphically displayed. Don't go far after you've entered the gate to the ampitheater compound. Look to your left and notice the gigantic white foot placed in the little fenced enclosure. This foot, which sports a remarkably good pedicure, is so large that it would put both Goliath and the Jolly Green Giant to shame. Most visitors to Caesarea get a "kick" out of being photographed in front of the foot.

In this area you will also see a grayish-white stone with an inscription. This is one of the

of his heart was only evil continually" (Genesis 6:5). Little has changed today.

North of Caesarea are the remains of a Roman aqueduct. Running parallel to the

Later, Dor was captured from the Philistines by David. Solomon awarded the city to Ben-Abinadab, his son-in-law (I Kings 4:7,11). And

Above: **The amphitheater of Caesarea**

City of Dor | was a purplish-red dye extracted from the mollusks that abounded along the Mediterranean coast. Only the rich, the nobility or the emperor could afford the expense of this purple dye.

North of Dor, but still nine miles south of Haifa, you will come to the ancient Phoenician port of ATLIT. Here you will see the impressive remains of the Crusader fortress Chateau de Pelerin—the Castle of the Pilgrims. Built in 1217-18 by the Templars, it was destroyed by the Baybars in 1291. The high wall of the citadel near the beach is most impressive. Unfortunately, the castle, fort and cathedral have been dismantled over the years so that the materials could be used to build breakwaters and basements throughout the Holy Land.

As you approach HAIFA, you can see why the city has been compared to San Francisco and Naples. It is precariously perched on

a hill, overlooking a sleepy bay.

Haifa, the third largest city in modern Israel, is both beautiful and unique. Its orientation is definitely vertical rather than horizontal. Like a club sandwich, Haifa climbs Mount Carmel on three levels. The lowest level is the port area, permeated with the sights, sounds and smells of the sea. The central level is called Hadar Ha Carmel, or Hadar for short. This is Haifa's business district. The highest level is the residential district on the mountain's peak. The view includes the city's colorful bay.

You will probably want to begin at the port, level one of the City of Haifa. The port area is pandemonium. The docks are piled high with crates of oranges, machines and the like. As you pass by the bazaar, you see merchants selling shish kebab and pita from oriental shops.

But there's more to this section of the city than first meets the eye. Near the docks is the Maritime Museum. Here you will find fascinating models of ancient Phoenician and Jewish sailing vessels, the kind built by <u>King Hiram of Tyre</u> and King Solomon of Jerusalem. Nearby are the huge grain elevators of Haifa and the Dagon Grain Silo. The archaeologi-

HAIFA: TRADE AND COMMERCIAL CENTER

The origin of Haifa is uncertain. The Crusaders called the site Caife, or Cayphe, and sometimes even Caiphas. This has led to speculation that the High Priest of Jerusalem in the days of Jesus may have been the founder. Others think the word Haifa may be a contracted form of the Hebrew words Hof Yafeh, meaning beautiful coast.

Haifa was inhabited by the ancient Phoenicians, as well as by Greeks and Jews, but it was destroyed by the Muslims in the seventh century. It was conquered by the Crusaders in 1100 and destroyed again in 1761. It wasn't until the twentieth century that the city really began to grow. The British constructed a harbor here in 1929 and turned Haifa into the trading and commercial center of Israel. More than a million and a half immigrant Jews disembarked here. Falling on Haifa's docks, they kissed the ground of their new Promised Land as they began their new life in Israel.

cal museum housed in this silo contains exhibits of ancient and modern methods of storing grain. Some samples of grain are 4000 years old.

To climb to level two, the Hadar, you must

tural engineering, civil and electrical engineering, mechanical and nuclear engineering and the like. The technology which went into building Solomon's Temple, Hezekiah's tun-

Above: City of Haifa

Below: Street in

DRAMA ON MOUNT CARMEL

Mount Carmel has always possessed a sort of religious sanctity. First Kings 18:30 records that this was the site of an altar of Jehovah. The prophet Elijah chose this site for his famous contest with the prophets of Baal (I Kings 18:19-39). When the 450 prophets of Baal were bested by the prophet of God, they were taken to Brook Kidron at the foot of the mountain and slain (I Kings 18:40). This small, reed-lined stream is quite unimpressive, but one day, thousands of years ago, it received the blood of the pagan prophets who mocked God and His servant.

The second site, located in a thick forest of trees, is the golden-domed Baha'i Temple, one of the most impressive structures in the Holy Land. From the street above, you get an excellent view—not only of the temple but of the Baha'i Shrine and Gardens as well. This temple is the world center of the Baha'i religion. Mirza Ali Mohammed, the forerunner of the Baha'i faith, is buried here. The gardens are immaculate and beautiful. The Corinthian-styled archives museum houses the historical records of the world's five million Baha'is.

And now, travel to level three, the top of Mount Carmel. Here the traditional site of the confrontation between the prophet Elijah and the prophets of Baal is marked by a Carmelite monastery.

The Carmel Range

The Carmel range is an outcropping of limestone mountains extending southeasterly some dozen miles inland and averaging 1500 feet in elevation. The range separates the Plain of Sharon from the Plain of Esdraelon. Carmel, which means "Vineyard of the Lord," has always been a biblical symbol of beauty and majesty (II Chronicles 26:10; Song of Solomon 7:5; Isaiah 35:2; Jeremiah 46:18; 50:19). Today it is the site of Israel's largest national park, which includes 25,000 acres of cypress, eucalyptus and pine trees.

ACRE

The road north to ACRE (also spelled Acco, Akko, and Accho) curves around the bay and clings to its shores. The city is picturesque, with tiny minarets set against a blue Mediterranean sky. As you enter the city along the sea wall, you will see the citadel, with its double walls and exceptionally deep moat.

When you enter it, a cold feeling comes over you, and you instinctively know you are in a prison. This citadel became the nation's central prison during the British mandate. After World War II it held hundreds of Jewish political prisoners. Today you can visit the English hanging-room where many of the

Israeli underground were put to death. If you descend to the dungeon, you will see the names of the Jewish freedom fighters inscribed on the walls. This infamous citadel is no longer a prison but the Museum Hagourah (which Pasha, its builder. The mosque is crowned by more than 40 white domes and a single minaret. The inside, which contains Jezzar's tomb, is gracefully decorated with oriental carpets and lavishly ornamented with red, the chief city of the territory of Asher, although it was never taken by this tribe (Joshua 19:24-31; Judges 1:31). It was incorporated into Israel during the reigns of David and Solomon, but it was returned to the Phoenicians as payment to King Hiram for the men and materials he provided to help build Jerusalem (I Kings 9:11-13; II Chronicles 8:1,2).

After the conquest of Tyre by Alexander the Great, Acre submitted to its conqueror, and its name was changed to Ptolemais. Emperor Claudius (A.D. 52-74) made it a Roman colony. The Crusaders arrived in 1104 and made Acre the principal port of the Holy Land. Saladin claimed the city in 1187, but Richard the Lion-Hearted reoccupied it four years later. In 1799, Napoleon besieged the city unsuccessfully, and this decisive defeat dashed his hopes for an Eastern Empire. Jezzar Pasha, whose cruelty earned him the nickname "the Butcher," strengthened the city's fortifications and built Acre's mosque and luxurious steam baths.

THE ROAD SOUTH
LOD (LYDDA)

Many who travel to Israel land at the country's largest airport, located at LOD. There you will find the Saint George Church. George, a patron saint of England, was believed to be a native son of Lod. He became a soldier in the Roman army and rebelled against the anti-Christian edicts of the Emperor Diocletian. He was martyred by the Romans and buried here in A.D. 303. The church marks the site.

Mentioned in Egyptian hieroglyphics 3500 years ago, Lod was a fortified town in Joshua's day and was built by Shamed, a Benjamite (I Chronicles 8:1,12; Nehemiah 11:13-35). It was apparently resettled after the Babylonian captivity (Ezra 2:1,33: Nehemiah 7:6,37). The Greeks changed its name to Lydda.

This is the city where Peter was used by God to heal Aeneas, the man who had been bedridden with the palsy for eight years (Acts 9:32-35). During the first Jewish revolt (A.D. 66-70) the city was demolished by the Roman armies on their way to Jerusalem. Later it became a center for Jewish scholarship and the permanent residence of the famed Rabbi Akiva and his academy.

ASHDOD

The journey south through the Coastal Plain must include the three coastal cities of the Philistines. First Samuel repeatedly tells us of the five lords of the Philistines and their five cities. While Ekron and Gath are inland cities and less important (their exact loca-

Refineries at Ashod

ASHDOD: LAUNCHPAD FOR PREACHING MINISTRY

Ashdod was an ancient Hyksos town which later became a Philistine stronghold. The name itself in Hebrew means "fortress." Little remains today of the biblical city, although the tell, or ancient ruin, is located three miles south of the mouth of the Lachish River on the Via Maris, a major north-south highway of antiquity. Excavations are underway at the site.

It was here that the Anakim lived, those giants of Joshua's day who prevented Israel from conquering Gaza, Gath, or Ashdod (Joshua 11:22). Although allotted to Judah, Ashdod was not taken (Joshua 13:1-3; 15:46,47). It was famous because it was the center of the worship of Dagon, an idol that was half fish and half man.

First Samuel 5 records the thrilling story of the Philistines capturing the ark of the covenant and bringing it to the house of Dagon in Ashdod. So powerful was the presence of Jehovah that every morning the people of Ashdod found Dagon flat on its face before the ark!

The paganism of this city was legendary. Nehemiah's indignation was aroused when the Jews intermarried with the Ashdodites (Nehemiah 13:23-24). Both Amos (Amos 1:8) and Zephaniah (Zephaniah 2:4) prophesied against the city.

With the coming of the Greeks, the city's name was changed to Azotus. In the irony of biblical history, this pagan city became the launching pad for a great preaching ministry. After Philip encountered the Ethiopian eunuch on the road to Gaza, Philip took an unexpected journey to Azotus. Acts 8:40 records, "But Philip was found at Azotus. And passing through, he preached in all the cities till he came to Caesarea."

tions are in dispute), the coastal cities of Ashdod, Ashkelon and Gaza are very noteworthy.

ASHDOD is growing furiously. High-rise

(fourteenth century B.C.) record that Ashkelon was a rich and rebellious city. A bas-relief carved picture at the temple of Pharaoh Ram-a favorite spot for Jewish picnickers. It is simply beautiful, one of the most restful spots in the troubled Middle East.

In fact, you can spread a blanket over the grass, lean against a 2000-year-old Roman column and just relax awhile. From this vantage point you can see the wonders of this unique combination of past and present. In the center of the park lie the foundations of several buildings. The remains of an ancient wall protrude from the sand, and three statues of the Goddess of Victory highlight these remains.

Take a stroll to the beach half a mile away. (Watch out for the Palestinian sun and the ubiquitous frisbees!) The granite pillars and rubble strewn across the mound overlooking the sea are all that remain of the old Philistine harbor.

Old Ashkelon, mentioned by Joshua (Joshua 13:3) and taken by the tribe of Judah (Judges 1:18), was rich and distinguished. So is new Ashkelon, with its tailored lawns and gardens. Old Ashkelon, where Samson slew 30 men (Judges 14:19) and where the ark was returned with a trespass offering (I Samuel 6:17), was the scene of frequently interrupted tranquility. So is new Ashkelon, where Israelis from all over the country flock for a summer vacation or a weekend getaway. Old Ashkelon, a city frequently chastised by Jehovah's prophets (Jeremiah 25:20; 47:6,7; Amos 1:8; Zephaniah 2:4,7), was an irreligious center of man-oriented activity. Little has changed.

GAZA

A kibbutz, YAD MORDECHAI, is about seven miles south of Ashkelon. It was established in 1943 and named in honor of Mordechai Anilevits, the leader of the Warsaw Ghetto re-

Roman pillars at Ashkelon Park

volt against the Nazis during World War II. The town is known for its strong defense against the advancing Egyptian armored divisions in 1948. A lifelike battlefield has been reconstructed there, with tanks and men realistically depicting that battle. Yad Mordechai is only two miles from the Gaza Strip border.

A word of warning: The Gaza Strip is an Israeli-occupied Arab territory in which twentieth-century tensions run high. You will probably not be permitted to enter the strip, due to "military reasons."

The more than 545,000 inhabitants of the Gaza Strip occupy an area 25 miles long and 3.6 miles wide. Since this area is administered by a military government, don't be surprised if your journey on the coastal road south stops at Ashkelon. From Acre to Ashkelon, the journey in the Holy Land is inspirational, informative, and intriguing. But above and below the coastal plain the journey becomes dangerous, and its only visitors are Israeli soldiers on patrol.

GAZA, which lies within the strip, is probably the oldest and most important of the five Philistine cities of antiquity. A prominent

REFLECTIONS: GAZA

Gaza has a somewhat idyllic setting, but it is in a hostile environment. You might expect it to be like a peaceful island in a belligerent sea. Just the opposite is true. Gaza has seen more than its share of bloodshed.

The exploits of Samson make this abundantly clear. To escape being killed by the Philistines, God's strongman carried the huge gates of Gaza all the way to Hebron, some 40 miles away (Judges 16:1-3). Still later, Samson was brought to Gaza after his seduction by Delilah. Here the Philistines gouged out his eyes and forced him to grind in the prison house (Judges 16:21). This is where Samson pulled down the pillars of the house of Dagon and killed more than 3000 in the process (Judges 16:23-30).

Alexander the Great captured this portal to Egypt in 332 B.C., killing all of Gaza's men and selling the women and children into slavery. This was the scene of many Christian martyrdoms. The British lost 10,000 men when they captured Gaza from the Turks. And here, in 1967, the Israeli

CHAPTER SIX

LAND OF THE NATIONS

UPPER AND LOWER GALILEE

"Now Jesus went about all Galilee, teaching in their synagogues, and preaching the gospel of the kingdom, and healing all kinds of sickness and all kinds of disease among the people."

Matthew 4:23

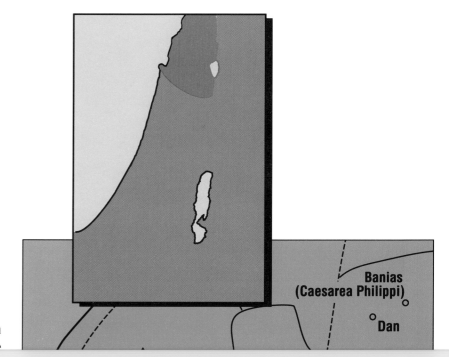

Banias
(Caesarea Philippi) ◦

◦ Dan

ALILEE is the northernmost region
of the Holy Land. Its boundaries are

JESUS AND THE GALILEANS

Galilee did not come into its own until New Testament times. In fact, it is mentioned only six times in the Old Testament. For the Christian, Galilee is important because it was the boyhood home of Jesus. He grew up in its lower hills. During the years of His earthly ministry He made several preaching tours throughout Galilee (Matthew 4:23-25; 9:35—10:15; 11:1-6). All but one of His disciples were Galileans. Our Lord prophetically announced His death, burial and resurrection from Galilee (Matthew 17:22,23); and from these hills He launched His journey to the cross (Matthew 19:1). Galilee was the rendezvous point for Jesus and His disciples after His resurrection; and here He gave them the Great Commission (Matthew 28:16-20).

In Bible times Galilee was separated from Judaea by Samaria, and it was completely surrounded by non-Jewish and frequently hostile populations. It is little wonder that the strict rabbis of Jerusalem distrusted the religious purity of the Galileans. Even Isaiah refers to them as "Galilee of the nations," indicating their distant position from the heart of the Jewish faith.

The Galileans were rough people, who resisted the Romans even more doggedly than did the Judeans; and they were considered uneducated, uncouth and unwieldy. Hence, Nathanael questioned whether any good thing could come out of Nazareth, one of the chief cities of Galilee (John 1:46). Ironically, after the fall of Jerusalem in A.D. 70, the rabbinic scholars and pietists flocked to Galilee in an attempt to maintain the Jewish religion.

Galilee is lush and green most of the year. It is a delight, a pageant of beauty, a tribute to God's love for this Holy Land.

UPPER GALILEE
CAESAREA PHILIPPI/BANIAS

The topography of northern Galilee is dominated by Mount Hermon. This majestic, snow-capped natural wonder rises 9232 feet above sea level. A sight of breathtaking beauty, its snowy crest is sometimes visible from as far away as Tel Aviv or the lower Jordan Valley. At the base of this mighty mountain is the main source of the Jordan River. Here, at BANIAS, where the river flows out of the ground, you can begin your journey southward through Galilee. (Banias, sometimes spelled Baniyas, was called Panias by the Greeks, who named it after Pan, the god of forests and flocks.)

As you approach the headwaters area, you'll be impressed with two things. The first is the beauty of the spot. It is one of the most gorgeous areas of the Middle East. Second, you'll immediately notice its coolness—especially if you visit in the summer. The thick foliage provides a protection from the heat of the summer sun, thus creating a pleasantly relaxing atmosphere for rest and refreshment. In fact, after many days of strenuous teaching, Jesus brought His disciples to this very spot to rest and pray (Luke 9:18).

On a hill adjacent to this Edenic paradise, Herod the Great built a temple to the god Pan in 20 B.C. After the death of Herod, his son, Philip, was awarded this region to rule

Right: **Mount Herman in the summer**

as a tetrarch (provincial governor). Philip erected a shrine to Caesar Augustus at this site and built a city, which he called CAESAREA PHILIPPI (a combination of Caesar's name and his own).

Along a winding path you'll see a gigantic, 100-foot-high cliff that is a part of a steep ridge. At its base, waters gush from a cave and bubble over the rock debris at the cave's entrance, becoming a peaceful and broad stream.

If you really want to be refreshed, don't use the little bridge over the stream to get to the cave. Take your shoes off and stone-hop the stream.

Just to the right of the cave you'll see three niches carved in the face of the cliff. The niches resemble tiny apses cut in the rock in an ascending pattern. The one near the top of the cave is the most perfect, and we presume that it held a statue at one time, probably of Pan.

This scenic arena is where Jesus asked His disciples, "Who do men say that I, the Son of Man, am?" Fully certain of his answer, Peter

DAN: BEAUTIFUL AND DANGEROUS

Dan is first mentioned in Scripture as the place to which Abraham pursued Chedorlaomer and his armies in order to rescue Lot (Genesis 14:13-16). The city was originally a Phoenician town named Laish (Judges 18:27-29) or Leshem (Joshua 19:47). It appears that the Danites, unsatisfied with their allotted territory in Judea (Joshua 19:40-47), decided to occupy this unclaimed area far to the north. They found it much as it is today, "very good

Son of the living God" (Matthew 16:13-16; Mark 8:27-30; Luke 9:18-21). Peter didn't need any statues or niches. He was in the presence of the Living God.

DAN

Four miles west of Banias is a second stream that is a source of the Jordan. Its copious waters flow into a luxuriant valley near the western base of a volcanic cone known as Tell Kedi. This mound is better known to Jews and Christians alike as DAN (Judges 18:29), the familiar Old Testament city that marked the northern limit of the Promised Land.

Dan is near the Lebanese border, and it is sometimes impossible to visit the city. When Middle East tensions rise, the diggers must sometimes abandon the archaeological dig and scurry to safer territory.

Both Banias and Dan, two of the four sources of the Jordan, were gorgeous gardens of dense vegetation and sparkling water. And both of them were the sites of pagan religious shrines. Do you see why pious Judeans looked upon the Galileans as spiritually degenerate (John 1:46)?

HAZOR

Your journey south to HAZOR will take you through the modern town of KIRYAT SHMONA ("city of eight"). Established only 20 years ago, this settlement was named in honor of eight valiant Jews who withstood an Arab attack at Tel Hai, just to the north. The settlement finds itself in the news today when occasional shelling from southern Lebanon occurs. Kiryat Shmona is usually first to receive the menacing missiles.

From here the road to Hazor skirts the western edge of the Hula Valley. Until 1950 there was a lake here called "Lake Hula." It was fed by the Jordan River, as are the Sea of Galilee and the Dead Sea. The lake was a vast marshland teeming with wildlife, water buffalo, wild boar, exotic birds and the like; but it was also a mosquito-infested swamp. During 1950 and 1951 the marshland was drained, leaving thousands of acres of very fertile soil. The Israelis

HAZOR: STRATEGIC CITY

Hazor has been inhabited for 4500 years and was once the largest city in Israel, with a population of more than 40,000. It is strategically located in a position to control the traffic moving through the Hula Valley. This has contributed to its importance—past and present.

Joshua knew he had to capture Jabin, king of Hazor, and his stronghold if he were to establish Israel in the land. He took the city and burned it to the ground (Joshua 11:1-14). Archaeologists have discovered the charred remains in the area north of the tell.

Later, a different king of Hazor, also named Jabin, possessed an army that had 900 iron chariots. He held dominion over Israel for 20 years. However, after Deborah challenged them, Barak and the armies of Israel defeated Sisera and the armies of Hazor in the Esdraelon Valley. We can read this amazing story in Judges 4. Many years later Solomon rebuilt Hazor as one of his chariot cities (I Kings 9:15).

have turned this land into productive farmland.

At the southern end of Hula Valley the highway runs just left of a huge mound of dirt. This is not a natural mound but a tell. "Tell" (Tel in Hebrew) is Arabic for an artificial mound that has been built up by successive levels of occupation. (It's like one mud pie piled on another mud pie, piled on another.) The highway winds around the tell very close to its base.

On this 25-acre rectangular plateau, archaeologists have identified 21 levels of occupation. This site was excavated by Professor Yigal Yadin and his archaeological team in 1955-58. Some interesting items remain here, especially the Hazor column rows. However, the artifacts have been removed to the museum of Kibbutz Ayelet Hashahar, near the base of the mound; and you can see them there. It's a fascinating museum—light, open and airy.

The climb to the top of Hazor offers a magnificent view of the Hula Valley. It's worthwhile, even if you aren't an archaeology buff.

Hazor has a water tunnel that dates back

Well at Hazor

were known as "Cabalists," because of their intricate system of applying a mystical interpretation to every sentence, word and letter

The delightful little village of Cana in Galilee

as the "charm city" of Israel.

Safed has now become an artists' colony. Just after you pass under the stone bridge, walk down the street to the right on the main street. Here you will find the Israeli Montmartre, home of sculptors, ceramists and painters. There you'll find old world charm in an ancient, yet modern, country.

Frankly, most Christians prefer simply to

NOBLEMAN'S SON HEALED

On the road entering Cana from the north, a bereaved nobleman received the most exciting news of his life. Having heard that Jesus was in Galilee, he had left a gravely ill son in Capernaum to seek Him out. He hoped the Master would come to Capernaum and heal him. Instead, Jesus spoke the miracle of healing and sent the nobleman back to Capernaum. On this road he met his servants who told him that his son was alive. The deadly fever had left him the same hour Jesus had spoken to the father in Cana (John 4:46-54).

look up at Safed from below. Despite all its history and medieval charm, still, Safed is an all-Jewish city, and it is not even mentioned in the Bible. However, when Jesus was teaching on the nearby Mount of Beatitudes, He said to His followers, "You are the light of the world. A city that is set on a hill cannot be hid" (Matthew 5:14). The Lord wants all who trust in Him to let their lights shine before a watching world so "that they may see your good works and glorify your Father in heaven" (Matthew 5:16). Most people believe that Jesus used the ancient city of Safed as an illustration of this truth. So, even if you don't enjoy the view of Galilee from Safed, enjoy the view of Safed from Galilee.

LOWER GALILEE
CANA

Nestled on the side of a lower Galilean mountain ridge is the city of CANA. As you approach the town, you are immediately dazzled by the brightness of the white buildings against the darker hillside. Cana is perhaps the most picturesque village in Galilee.

There is still some debate as to whether or

The city is never mentioned in the Old Testament, nor is it found on most ancient maps. As we approach the city, the hairpin turns on the road provide a delightful opportunity to view Nazareth from a variety of angles.

Nazareth consists of two cities, rather than two levels of the same city. The lower city, the biblical town in which Jesus grew up, is the largest Arab community in Israel—apart from the Arab quarters in Jerusalem. Some 52,000 Arabs live here, about half of them Christian With more than 40 convents, monasteries, orphanages, churches and private schools, Nazareth is the undisputed headquarters of the Christian mission movement in Israel. In 1957 the Upper Nazareth suburb of Kiryat Natsrat was established on the top of the mountain by Jewish immigrants from Eastern Europe. The New City, with a population of more than 25,000, is almost exclusively Jewish.

Our interest is in the Old City. It contains a maze of Christian sites, mostly housed in white buildings under brown or orange roofs. Some would say that the most important church in Nazareth is the Church of the Annunciation. You can't miss it. Its large polygonal tower, which slopes at a steep pitch upward,

not this is the Cana of the New Testament. Nonetheless, this village, tucked in the folds of the hills four miles north of Nazareth, is commemorated as that city.

As you come into town from the north, you pass a small chapel, the Saint Nathanael

JESUS IN NAZARETH

Nazareth's importance is inextricably linked to the life of Jesus. We can easily imagine how in Nazareth "Jesus increased in wisdom and stature, and in favor with God and men" (Luke 2:51,52). The boy Jesus must have romped and played with His friends on the surrounding hills. From the peaks above the town He could look southward and see the trade caravans on their way to Egypt. He would observe "the lilies of the field," watch the new-mown grass wither in the hot August sun, and follow the rhythm of the men as they sowed or winnowed grain. Do you recall His mentioning these things? "One will be taken and the other left" (Matthew 24:41) probably came from his memories of the Nazarene women grinding meal at the circular stone mill.

Nazareth was a tiny hamlet, perched above the broad valley below. Nevertheless, its environs provided the young Nazarene with a myriad of sights and sounds from which he drew anecdotes and parables during His earthly ministry.

Jesus could easily walk to the neighboring town of SEPHORIS (Diocasarea), the Roman administrative center of Galilee. Here He could mingle with the rich and the poor, the proud and the humble, the pious and the profane.

rises impressively above the buff-white masonry church. The tower resembles an Apollo space vehicle, perched atop a stubby Saturn rocket. The best angle for a picture of this basilica is from the road above the church.

The Latin Church of the Annunciation is located on Casa Nova Street. It stands on the spot where, according to tradition, the angel Gabriel appeared to the virgin Mary and announced that she had been chosen by God to bear the Christ-child (Luke 1:26). Completed in the 1960's, the church was built on the site of a Franciscan church that was erected in 1730. That church, in turn, had been built over a Crusader church. At one end of the church you will see a cave. This grotto marks the sacred site where the angel is said

Almost anything can be bought in the sidewalk shops of Nazareth.

to have appeared to Mary. Two granite pillars mark the spots where the angel Gabriel and the virgin may have stood at the annunciation.

Next to the Latin church, adjacent to the Franciscan Convent, is the Church of St. Joseph. The two caves under this church are said to have housed Joseph's carpenter's shop and the storage room. Although you won't see any carpenter's tools here now, your nose will be treated to the delightful smell of wood-shavings and sawdust from a modern carpenter's workbench nearby. This carpenter fashions wooden ploughs and tools for the Arab farmers who work the neighboring fields.

Don't leave Nazareth until you have absorbed some local Arab color. Wander down one of the narrow, crowded, cobblestone streets that sprout from Casa Nova like the legs from a centipede. You are in for a real treat. Let your nose be your guide through the highly aromatic (I use the word in the worst possible sense) marketplace. You will have to sidestep donkeys, waterpot-bearing women and large piles of garbage as you snake your way through the streets. But the adventure is well worth the adversity. Steer clear of the two-foot-wide trench running down the center of the street. This is the city's sewage system.

Tin-roofed shops line the narrow streets.

These add new meaning to the concept of "cramped" quarters. The stalls outside the shops contain inviting fruit. Inside, you'll find hardware, leather goods, ancient coins, glassware, clothes, rope—and just about anything else your heart desires. Side by side hang trash and treasures. In one smelly opening you'll see plastic buckets and sponges hanging from the roof; in the next, authentic archaeological artifacts are on sale at inflated prices. The deeper you venture into the Arab market, the smaller the shops become; but the smaller the shops become, the lower the prices become.

On the road toward Tiberias you will find the Greek Orthodox Church of the Annunciation, or Gabriel's Church. This church was originally built in the days of Constantine and is a rival to the newer Latin Church of the Annunciation. The present structure is more than 300 years old, the oldest church in Nazareth. Inside this dark and gloomy structure, an Orthodox priest will show you a spring which bubbles out of the hillside below the floor. Steps lead down to the original well. It is believed that here Mary came to draw water, perhaps accompanied by the boy Jesus. Since this is the only spring-fed fountain in Nazareth, there is a good chance this stream provided cooling refreshment for the Lord Jesus.

Outside, by the side of the road, you'll see the round-faced masonry well known as Mary's Well, or the Virgin's Fountain. This is an outlet for the spring which originates below the church. Before the water was piped to the residences of the town, Nazarene women would come here daily to get water for their families. You may yet see a woman carrying water home, just as Mary did for Joseph and Jesus; but today she will carry it in four-gallon jars or shiny tin containers.

While you're in Nazareth, you may want to visit the old synagogue in the western part of town on Market Lane. According to tradition, this ancient synagogue is where Jesus "went into the synagogue on the Sabbath day, and stood up to read" (Luke 4:16), astounding those present. You may also want to drive by the Hill of the Precipice ("Leap of the Lord") southeast of the city. It is believed that this sharp, tree-dotted hill is the cliff over which the enraged townspeople of Nazareth tried to throw our Lord (Luke 4:28-30). The most impressive view of this steep hill is from the road running parallel to it. There you will see the craggy cliff against the clear blue of the Palestinian sky.

As you leave the city of Jesus' youth, the words of Nathanael may ring in your ears: "Can any good thing come out of Nazareth?" (John 1:46). Jesus proved that adage wrong.

VALLEY OF ARMAGEDDON

The Plain of Esdraelon stretches below Nazareth, the crown jewel of the Galilee hills. Commonly called the Emek, this Jezreel Valley is known to Christians as the VALLEY OF ARMAGEDDON. The largest and most fertile valley in Israel, the Esdraelon lies between the Galilee hills on the north and the hills of Samaria on the south. On the west is Mount Carmel; on the east, Mount Gilboa. Until the early 1920's this was a mosquito-ridden, malarial swampland; but the Jewish National Fund inaugurated its largest land reclamation project ever and transformed it into the most beautiful valley in the world. Its patchwork of greens and golds soothes the eyes and stirs the soul.

The small entrance to Gabriel's Church and the bubbling spring that feeds Mary's Well

MOUNT TABOR

This symmetrical Mount Tabor is the boundary between Issachar and Zebulun (Joshua 19:22,23). Deborah and Barak met here before defeating Sisera (Judges 4:6-17). Here, too, Zebah and Zalmunna slew Gideon's brothers (Judges 8:18-21). As early as the fourth century A.D., the tradition that this rounded mountain was the site of Jesus' transfiguration had become established. But many Christians believe that the description of the Mount of Transfiguration as "a high mountain" (Matthew 17:1; Mark 9:2; Luke 9:28) more naturally fits Mount Hermon than Mount Tabor.

THE PLAIN OF ESDRAELON

This is Esdraelon. This is Jezreel. This is Armageddon. Here Gideon and his 300 men were victorious (Judges 7). Here King Josiah was mortally wounded in battle (II Chronicles 35:20-24). Elijah ran some 20 miles down this valley from Mount Carmel ahead of King Ahab's chariot (I Kings 18:46).

The armies of the Egyptians, Philistines, Assyrians, Persians, Greeks, Romans, Crusaders, Turks and British have tramped through these prosperous fields. And the armies keep coming. (A young Israeli paratrooper once told me he parachuted into this valley on a training mission, only to land rather messily in a watermelon patch.)

In Revelation 16:13-16, the Apostle John describes the greatest battle ever to take place in the valley—the Battle of Armageddon (Revelation 16:13-16). As you view the tiny agricultural towns and settlements glistening in the Esdraelon sun, and as you look across the fruitful fields of grain waving in the breeze, it is difficult to imagine this as a plain of ghost towns and blood-soaked fields. But the Word of God stands sure.

A ten-minute ride along the main road, west from Nazareth and through the valley, brings you to the turnoff to NAHALAL. Among the earliest of Israeli settlements, Nahalal is the most photographed moshav (individually owned cooperative community). From the air the moshav looks like a wagon wheel with farms at the hub and quaint white houses at the rim. Rows and rows of trees and country lanes radiate between the two. Tailored fields flare out from the houses. It is here that the late Israeli soldier-statesman,

Moshe Dayan, is buried.

The magnificent ruins of BEIT SHEARIM lie a few miles farther west and to the left of the highway. These ruins remained untouched until a quarter of a century ago. Their excavation and restoration has brought fresh insight into the development of the Jewish religion after the destruction of the Jerusalem Temple in A.D. 70.

Near the ruins of a large synagogue you'll find a grove of olive and cypress trees. Many learned and famous Jews are buried in the extensive catacombs in this grove.

The entrance to the burial caves is through the rock-hewn door under the arches at the back of the courtyard. Inside these cool shelters are sarcophagi beautifully carved with menorahs, rams' horns, the ark, lions and shells. Many of the 200 important sarcophagi have been looted by grave robbers over the years. There's an item of special interest at the entrance to one of the inner burial chambers—a carving of a menorah, the Jewish seven-stemmed candelabrum. You'll see it high on the wall. The broad hallways of this city of the dead are much more easily traversed than are their counterparts in the Roman Catacombs.

Another road from Nazareth strikes out due south across the Plain of Esdraelon toward AFULA. As you look to your left, you will see a bowl-shaped mountain with a concentration of trees near the top—Mount Tabor.

As you drive across the heart of the Valley of Armageddon, look left and right; and you will see the fertile Jezreel Valley, the breadbasket of Israel. Brilliant flowers, golden grain, green vegetables and rich black dirt are visible on all sides. These crops are brought to the rapidly developing market town of Afula for distribution.

Almost in the center of the valley, Afula serves as the administrative headquarters of Jezreel. Although it is located on the site of a Crusader fortress and one of Napoleon's victories, Afula was established only recently. It was pioneered in 1925, mostly by American Jews.

MEGIDDO

MEGIDDO, once a royal city of the Canaanites, lies on the extreme southern edge of the Jezreel Valley. It is strategically located at the pass through the Carmel Mountain range and leads from the Plain of Sharon on the coast to the Plain of Esdraelon.

MEGIDDO:
THE SITE OF MOMENTOUS EVENTS

As the Gibraltar of Palestine, Megiddo guarded one of the most important highways of the Ancient Near East—the road between Egypt and Asia.

Pharaoh Thutmose III conquered Megiddo, overpowering the Canaanite kings in 1468 B.C. His escapades are recorded on the walls of his palace in Karnak, Egypt. Pharaoh Necho's armies marched through the pass at Megiddo and were challenged by Judah's King Josiah. The young monarch's death in the ensuing battle was a crushing blow to the kingdom of Judah (II Kings 23:29,30).

Alexander the Great came this way in his pursuit of conquering the world. Vespasian's armies marched here. Napoleon led his army north from Egypt through this pass to an embarrassing defeat at Acre. Allenby came through here in 1917, and Jewish tanks rumbled by Megiddo on June 6, 1967.

An archaeologist's dream—the ancient Tell Megiddo

You will not want to miss the Megiddo museum. The site, with its beautifully manicured gardens, is developed and maintained by Israel's National Parks Authority. Once inside, there is not only relief from the heat of the day but refreshment for the parched tongue.

Here you can purchase some of the most useful souvenirs from the Holy Land. Of special interest are the brass menorahs, Torah scrolls and bottle openers.

Take your time in the museum. It is best to enter the door at the right corner and absorb the museum before you attack the mound. The oversized photos of the Megiddo excavations tell the real story of the pains and pleasures of participating in an archaeological dig. In the far room is a model of the Megiddo mound. It shows the more than 20 successive levels of occupation on this site. Take careful note of the shape of the mound, the steep entranceway on the far side and the intricate gate system. In just a few moments you'll be conquering that entranceway yourself. Periodically since 1903, Megiddo has fallen under the archaeologist's spade. The results have provided outstanding validation of the Old Testament.

Now you can climb the Megiddo mound. At the top of the ascent you make a sharp left turn. This turn was designed so that charging chariots could not negotiate this part of the gate system. This simple architectural maneuver added significantly to Megiddo's security.

Stay on the stone-lined path. You soon come to a right-hand turn. Here you will see a perfect example of a stone manger and wa-

tering trough—one square and one round. These are similar to those used in Solomon's day. During his reign, this city was one of the most fortified defense posts in his vast empire. First Kings 10:26 indicates that Solomon gave whole cities over to the stabling of the horses of his cavalry. Megiddo is mentioned as one of them.

Ahead, where the path forks to the right, you'll find an area where archaeologists have uncovered stables large enough to house 450 horses and 150 chariots. There, too, you'll see mangers and watering troughs. Archaeologists have identified these as King Ahab's (874-853 B.C.). However, Solomon's stables would have been similar—if these are not his.

Now take the path that leads to the edge of the mound that overlooks the Jezreel Valley. Behind you is a crater with a large circular Canaanite altar at its center. This is perhaps the best view of the actual archaeological excavations at Megiddo. As you approach the mound's ridge, treat your eyes to a spine-tingling sight—the Valley of Armageddon.

To leave the mound of Megiddo, you may retrace your steps down the steep entranceway or you may exit through an ancient marvel of engineering—the Megiddo water tunnel. I suggest the latter. On the far side of the

mound is a circular depression. If it weren't for the faint traces of long-unused steps clinging to the side, you would think this depression is but a mysterious sinkhole. Yet this is the opening to the Megiddo water system, which dates back 2800 years.

As you enter the cave-like mouth, you descend on a system of metal steps. Watch the steps; they can be difficult. Once you reach the base of the shaft you will be 120 feet below the surface. There you'll see an ingeniously carved tunnel, 215 feet long, that connects with a spring outside the city. Your feet will remain dry as you walk on the four-foot-wide wooden boardwalk that leads to the opposite end. You will soon ascend the metal stairs and arrive on the back side of the mound.

AROUND THE SEA OF GALILEE

Much of the ministry of our Lord Jesus took place on and around the Sea of Galilee. Some of Galilee's most important towns are located on its shores. Let's pretend that the sea is the clock and Bethsaida is at high noon. In a counterclockwise fashion you will travel

Above: Megiddo water tunnel

Left: Model of ancient Megiddo

ARMAGEDDON

As you look out over this vast valley, the scene of so many conflicts in the past, it's hard to believe that the quilted field below will be the scene of history's final and bloodiest battle. Yet, five reliable authors record this great battle on the sacred pages of the Bible. They are David, Isaiah, Joel, Zechariah and John. Read Psalm 2:1-5,9; Isaiah 34:1-6; 63:3-6; Joel 3:2,9-16; Zechariah 12:2; 14:2,3,12; and Revelation 14:14-20; 16:16; 19:11-21. In the valley before you, God will gather the nations together in a battle that will extend to the Valley of Jehoshaphat at Jerusalem and all the way to Moab. "And they gathered them together to the place called in Hebrew, Armageddon" (Revelation 16:16). The name means "the mound of Megiddo." This judgment of God on the nations of the world results from the godlessness of the last days, but God will be victorious. He always is.

southward from where the Jordan River empties into the Sea of Galilee near Bethsaida to Degania at six o'clock, where the Sea of Galilee empties into the Jordan River.

SEA OF GALILEE

Of the five main roads that lead to the Sea of Galilee, the road from Nazareth offers the most impressive view. As you drive over the Galilean hills toward the sea, you descend into a dip in the road and head up the other side. Suddenly, there it is—the Sea of Galilee.

This sea fills a depression between the hills of Galilee and the heights of Golan. Historically it was nearly 700 feet below sea level and averaged 130-157 feet deep. Its area was about 64 square miles, with the sea holding approximately 141 billion cubic feet of water. The distance from the point where the Jordan River flowed into Galilee to the point where it flowed out again was a little more than 13 miles. Its width was half that size. Over the years a lack of rainfall and excessive pumping for agricultural irrigation have drastically reduced the size of the lake and its water level.

Israel today has only two large inland bodies of water (since Lake Hula was drained). One is the Sea of Galilee; the other is the Dead Sea. One is fresh water; the other is salt water. In the Sea of Galilee fish are abundant. Sardine, mullet, catfish, carp, and six varieties of Cichlidae mouth-breeders, including the popular St. Peter's Fish, are all caught there. These are the same kinds of fish once caught by Jesus' disciples.

One of the great thrills of being in the Holy Land is taking a boat ride on the Sea of Galilee. Usually the trip begins at the docks of Tiberias, and the boat carries you across to Capernaum on the north. As the boat backs away from the dock, you will see an army of little children who have gathered on the shore. They are there to wave and smile and spread their own brand of Galilean good cheer.

Once you set out across the water, you get a perfect view of the now infamous GOLAN HEIGHTS on your right. This tableland east and north of the Sea of Galilee was assigned to the tribe of Manasseh (Deuteronomy 4:43;

Joshua 20:8). At the end of World War I these mountains were awarded to Syria.

The Syrian bombardment of EIN GEV on the eastern lakefront precipitated the Six Day War in 1967.

As you cross the sea you can almost hear Jesus say to Peter, "Launch out into the deep and let down your nets for a catch" (Luke 5:4). Besides fish, tiny shells that are conical in shape abound. The captain of your boat and his crew will undoubtedly have a supply of these shells crafted into beautiful pins and brooches. A pin with dozens of these tiny shells symmetrically arranged makes a delightful and an inexpensive gift.

By the time you have gone halfway across the sea, the famous HORNS OF HATTIN become clearly visible on your left. This ridge, which is seven and one-half miles west of Tiberias, has an odd configuration that resembles the horns of an animal. Hence the name.

During the period of the Crusades,the Muslims had overrun Palestine, and the Christian Crusaders were trying to reclaim it. The conflict between the two forces came down to one final battle. Here, at the Horns of Hattin, the Crusaders suffered their final devastating defeat at the hands of Saladin in

THE SEA OF GALILEE

Don't be surprised if you see the Sea of Galilee listed under a variety of names on maps. In olden days the Arab poets called it "The Bride," "The Silver Woman" and "The Handmaiden of the Hills." In the King James Version of the Bible it is known as "Chinnereth" (Numbers 34:11; Joshua 12:3; 13:27). The modern spelling is "Kinneret," which is taken from the Hebrew word Kinnor, meaning "lute" or "harp." The sea is roughly harp-shaped. In the New Testament it is sometimes called "Gennesaret" (Luke 5:1).

After Herod Antipas built Tiberias on its western shore, the sea's most common designation was the "Sea of Tiberias" (John 6:1,23; 21:1). But it was also affectionately known as the "Sea of Galilee" (Matthew 4:18; 15:29; Mark 1:16; 7:31; John 6:1).

Have you ever wondered why a relatively small body of fresh water is called a sea? The answer lies in the configuration of the mountains around the sea. With the high mountains on either side, the tunneling wind whistles down from the north across the surface of the water, churning a placid lake into a howling sea. Crosswinds from the Mediterranean blow past the Horns of Hattin on the west and stir up the water. The incident in Mark 6:45-52, where a sudden and violent storm arose and just as quickly was calmed at the Master's command, presents a classic example of this natural phenomenon.

The tribe of Gad settled along the shore of this sea after the conquest of the land (Deuteronomy 3:17; Joshua 13:27,28). On the northern shores of Galilee Jesus called Peter, Andrew, James and John to leave their fishing business, follow Him and become fishers of men (Luke 5:1-11). Along these shores multitudes were healed (Luke 9:1-6), multitudes were fed (Luke 9:10-17) and multitudes were taught (Luke 9:23-27,37-62). On the eastern shore Jesus cast the demons out of the demoniac and into the swine (Matthew 8:28-34).

The Horns of Hattin

1187. The Crusades were over, and the Christian influence was then gone from Palestine.

Before you dock at Capernaum be sure to look ahead and a bit to the right at the huge mountain range towering to the clouds. This is the Anti-Lebanon Mountain range. The snowcapped peak is Mount Hermon. Nearly 20 miles long, north to south, and about 9200 feet high, Mount Hermon is the highest and the most spectacular mountain in the Middle East. Its snowy crown is white year-round. This mountain range was the northern limit of the territory of Israel (Deuteronomy 4:47, 48; Joshua 11:1-3; 12:1-5; 13:5).

When you dock at Capernaum, you will have spent 45 minutes on the Sea of Galilee. On this short trip you will have been taken back in time to the days when Jesus conducted His ministry on the shores of this sea.

When you have viewed these sites from the sea, you may want to retrace His steps on land.

CAPERNAUM

CAPERNAUM is located about two and one-half miles west of where the Jordan River feeds the Sea of Galilee. If we were to set out overland, cross the Jordan and travel east another mile and a half, we would come to

the ruins of Tel Beit Zaida. Situated 100 feet higher than the sea, this site is believed to be the biblical BETHSAIDA.

Capernaum features by far the most impressive ruins of the three cursed cities. Due to the shallowness of the Sea of Galilee, a new dock has been constructed west of the city for those who cross the sea by boat. Whether you enter the city from the sea or from the highway that hugs the shore from Tiberias, all you can see is a clump of trees, partially-excavated ruins and a huge black basalt building at the entrance of the city (the Franciscan Monastery).

The archaeological site is anything but dead. It is alive with activity. Over the years, especially during the 1980's, a lone Franciscan monk/archaeologist has managed the incredible feat of excavating the entire ruins. He has dug out and cataloged finds and then refilled the ruins with dirt. What remains of the city is seen in the ancient synagogue and in the notable artifacts that are stored around the perimeter of the excavation esplanade.

As you walk along in the coolness provided by the trees, notice that the pieces of black basalt stone on display are beautifully and intricately carved. Rosettes, fruit, candelabra and even a star of David are depicted. The variety is fascinating. But there is one carving you absolutely must see. Look toward the

THE CITY OF BETHSAIDA

This city was the birthplace of Peter, Andrew, James, John and Philip (Luke 5:10; John 1:44). The feeding of the 5000 took place on the grassy fields between the city and the sea (Matthew 14:13-21; John 6:1-14).

Jesus took the blind man out of this city and healed him (Mark 8:22-26). Perhaps He did this because of the unbelief of the people (Matthew 11:21,22). Regardless, Jesus cursed Bethsaida because it failed to repent of its sin and believe His message (Luke 10:13,14). He cursed the adjacent cities of Capernaum and Chorazin as well, and all three of them lie in ruins today. On the other hand, Tiberias was not cursed by the Lord, and it thrives today.

lake side of the esplanade. There you will see a very detailed replica of the ark of the covenant, sculpted in stone. This bas-relief shows a pillared chest mounted on six-spoked wheels. It looks not unlike an ornate Conestoga wagon or stage coach of early America. Don't miss it. It's one of the very few ancient representations of the ark known today.

The beautiful and modern church erected at the southeast corner of the esplanade is of recent vintage, and it marks the site of Peter's home in Capernaum. Presumably it was here that Peter's mother-in-law was healed by the Lord Jesus (Luke 4:38,39). While the architecture of the church is striking, somehow the whole building seems out of place in these ancient ruins.

The synagogue lies at the northeast corner of Capernaum. The present structure bears the telltale design of Roman architecture and is one of the finest limestone synagogues in the Middle East.

When the Franciscan fathers began reconstruction on the site in the last century, the only things still in place—from the fourth- or fifth-century edifice—were the lower three or

four courses of the walls, the column bases and the paved floor. They had to reposition and restore everything else. This was likely the site of the first-century Jewish center of worship where Jesus taught (Mark 1:21; Luke 4:31-33). If you know Latin, you may want to try to read the Roman inscriptions on some of the four columns that are still standing.

As you walk back toward the iron gate entrance, take note of several additional sites.

Above: Stone relief of the ark of covenant

Below: The Capernaum synagogue

CAPERNAUM: JESUS' OWN CITY

Capernaum became Jesus' "own city" after He withdrew from Nazareth (Matthew 4:13-17). It was the headquarters for His Galilean ministry, and the ancient synagogue was the central focus of that ministry.

It was here that He taught (Mark 1:21; Luke 4:31-33).

It was here that He healed:

The man with an unclean spirit and Peter's mother-in-law
    (Luke 4:31-41)

The centurion's servant (Luke 7:1-10)

The palsied man let down through the roof (Mark 2:1-12)

The woman who had an issue of blood
    (Luke 8:43-48)

The blind-and-dumb demoniac (Matthew 9:27-33)

The man with the withered hand (Luke 6:6-10)

The nobleman's son (John 4:46-54)

In fact, great multitudes were brought to Jesus and healed in this town (Matthew 8:16-17; 9:35-38).

One wonders, *What stories could the stones beneath this synagogue floor tell?*

Just west of the synagogue, along the northern edge of the esplanade, you can see a Via Maris milestone. Nearby is a first-century A.D. mosaic of a boat. This once decorated a house in the Galilee seaside town of Migdal.

A perfectly preserved olive press stands at the northwest corner of the esplanade. The millstone of this press is tipped on its side to give us a better view. The stone is made of black basalt (a volcanic stone native to the shores of Galilee). This is the same type of stone that was used to construct the Franciscan monastery. The millstone is a photographer's dream—a huge black stone against a background of flowers and trees.

This stone is more than two feet in diameter and more than a foot thick. Seeing it helps us better appreciate what Jesus meant when He said that rather than offend a little child it would be better for a man to have a millstone hung upon his neck and to be drowned in the depth of the sea (Matthew 18:6). Jesus said this at Capernaum. Could this be the millstone He used to illustrate His teaching?

CHORAZIN

When you take the lake road west from Capernaum, within two miles you will notice a branch road veering sharply to the right, away from the sea. This road climbs steeply. Within two or three miles you will see the spur leading to CHORAZIN, a Jewish center of the second century A.D.

Excavations undertaken at Chorazin between 1962 and 1965 revealed an old third- or fourth-century synagogue. In the 1980's, it was decided to include Chorazin in Israel's national park system. This provided an opportunity for further excavation. Two domestic complexes and a religious complex were unearthed. The latter featured a large mikveh or ritual bath, at the bottom of a seven-step entryway. But the major "must-see site" is the once elegant synagogue of carved basalt stone.

Generally, Chorazin is quite overgrown with briars and brush, and it is a haven for lizards. It stands as mute testimony to the judgment

It is built partially of black basalt rock and has a black dome on top of a square pavilion that is supported by arched colonnades trimmed in white.

The interior decor of the chapel depicts the seven virtues: charity, justice, providence, faith, hope, fortitude and temperance (Galatians 5:22). These remind you of the themes of the Sermon on the Mount. There are many terrific views of the Sea of Galilee, but none is better than the one you can see from the colonnaded walkway around the exterior of the chapel. The panorama takes your breath away.

While visiting this site, I have always found it spiritually revitalizing to slip off by myself under one of the multitude of trees and read Matthew 5—7, the Sermon on the Mount. It can be done in only a few minutes. As I read, I always find it difficult to keep my eyes on the pages of my Bible. They want to drift to the beautiful scenery surrounding me. So many of the things the Lord mentions in that sermon can still be seen around this mountain today.

TABGHA

When you descend the Mount of Beatitudes, you will rejoin the main road where the Galilean hills gently line the highway as you travel toward the sea. The village of

of God. You can almost hear Jesus' ringing indictment, "Woe to you, Chorazin! Woe to you, Bethsaida! For if the mighty works which were done in you had been done in Tyre and Sidon, they would have repented long ago in sackcloth and ashes" (Matthew 11:21).

MOUNT OF BEATITUDES

Go back now to the road that follows the Sea of Galilee. There you can visit the spot where Jesus delivered the Sermon on the Mount. It's a pleasant place, a place where you can relax; and it reminds you of a forest.

As you approach the site, on your left you will see a large Italian convent and The Hospice of the Beatitudes. This hospice is operated by an Italian missionary society and was a personal project of Mussolini in 1937.

A right turn (toward the sea) takes you through a grove of palm trees to the beautiful and picturesque Chapel of the Beatitudes.

TABGHA lies before you. Here you will find the bland-looking Church of the Multiplication. It stands on the site where tradition says Jesus fed the 5000. However, the Bible places this miracle near Bethsaida, east of the Jordan River (Luke 9:10). Nonetheless, this is a significant stop in any Holy Land itinerary. The church has one of the best preserved mosaics in Palestine.

The present building was reconstructed and dedicated in 1982. You will enter it through the rear. On its perimeters, the mosaic floor of an older church that dates back to the fourth century A.D. is visible. The magnificent tiles of this mosaic were discovered in 1932. The designs are of wildlife and flowers. And you will be able to discern a dove on a lotus flower, a bird attacking a snake, a goose with an oleander bush, as well as swans, cranes, wild geese and storks. How well this testifies to the flourishing nature of the Holy Land during those centuries.

At the front of the church there is a spendid Byzantine mosaic—one of the most beautiful I've seen. It depicts a basket of loaves with an upright fish on either side. This is an almost perfect mosaic and appears as if it were done only yesterday. It is a fitting commemoration of Jesus' great miracle.

Next door, along the seashore, is Saint Peter's Church, or the Mensa Christi ("Table of Christ"). This little basalt church was erect-ed by the Franciscans in 1943 on the ruins of an earlier church. Both were built over a massive rock called the "Table of Christ." It is believed that this is where Jesus prepared the breakfast of fish and bread for His disciples after His resurrection (John 21:9-14). The Lord Jesus' invitation to them is His invitation to all who experience physical or spiritual hunger: "Come and eat" (John 4:13,14; 6:47-51). This is also where Jesus commanded Peter three times, "Feed my sheep" (John 21:15,16,17). Responsibility always follows refreshment.

As you leave Tabgha, you will cross the Plain of Gennesaret. The highway never strays far from the shoreline. Soon you will pass the famous KINNERET PUMPING STATION, on the left.

GINOSSAR

Just before you arrive at Magdala, you pass a fine example of an Israeli phenomenon—the kibbutz. Kibbutzim are remarkable experiments in voluntary socialism. Everything is owned in common, and all the services of the community are provided in common.

At KIBBUTZ GINOSSAR is the Nof Ginossar Guest House, which is very popular and convenient—only minutes from downtown Tiberias. It is situated right on the sea and it has private beaches and gardens. One hundred and six rooms, with all the modern

Opposite: **The Sea of Galilee from the Chapel of the Beatitudes**

Left: **Byzantine mosaic of loaves and fish**

Below: **Saint Peter's Church at Tabgha**

conveniences, await weary travelers. The view of the Sea of Galilee from the second-story kosher dining room is fantastic. If you're interested in learning more about life on a kibbutz, a regular series of lectures and slides is provided by the resident kibbutzniks. It is a delightful and restful stop.

The Galilee Boat

In 1985 and 1986 a severe drought gripped Israel. The winter rains barely came, and the water level in the lake decreased drastically. Moshe and Yuval Lufan lived with their families on Kibbutz Ginossar. Avid amateur archaeologists, they frequently explored the newly exposed lake bed for ancient remains. In January of 1986 their efforts paid off.

A wheel of a tractor became stuck in the mud and churned up some ancient bronze coins. The brothers quickly discovered the oval outline of a boat that was entirely submerged in the wet mud. They decided to consult Mendel Nun, the local expert on the

Kinneret. He, in turn, notified the Department of Antiquities.

The boat was excavated. Immediately it was deemed a treasure. The planks of the hull were joined with the mortise-and-tenon type of joint, a rare method of holding planks in place with wooden pegs. (Examples of this method date back to the fourteenth century B.C.) The boat was painstakingly removed from the mud and placed in a holding tank near the Yigal Allon Museum at Ginossar. The tank contained a synthetic wax called polyethylene glycol, which filled the cellular cavities of the deteriorated wood. This wax now preserves THE GALILEE BOAT.

Measuring 26 1/2 feet long and 7 1/2 feet wide, the boat is 4 1/2 feet high and looks remarkably like the boat potrayed in the first-century A.D. mosaic in Capernaum. By submitting it to the Carbon 14 dating process, experts have estimated that this fishing vessel dates from somewhere between 120 B.C. and A.D. 40. That means that the Galilee Boat may well have been a craft similar to that used by Peter, Andrew, James and John. It's definitely worth a visit to the Yigal Allon Museum to see it.

MAGDALA

A mile south is MAGDALA, believed to be the home of Mary Magdalene (Mark 16:9; Luke 8:2).

It was to Magdala that our Lord came after the feeding of the 4000 (Matthew 15:39).

After the crowds dispersed, some of His antagonists asked for a sign from heaven. He responded, "When it is evening you say, 'It will be fair weather, for the sky is red'; and in the morning, 'It will be foul weather today, for the sky is red and threatening.' Hypocrites! You know how to discern the face of the sky, but you cannot discern the signs of the times" (Matthew 16:2,3).

Jesus often used visible objects and real-life situations to illustrate His teaching. As you look out over the Plain of Gennesaret to the west and the Sea of Galilee to the east, and as you have occasion to see the beauti-

ful sunrises and sunsets in that area, you can use your imagination and see Jesus as He dealt with the hypocrites. He must have looked out over the Sea of Galilee and then, pointing to the skies, rebuked them for their inability to accept His teaching.

The name "Magdala" means "tower." It was a city of some significance in the Greco-Roman Empire because of its position at the juncture of two main highways. It was apparently the most important town on the lake before Tiberias was built.

Josephus, the first-century A.D. Jewish historian, notes that the city had a population of 40,000 (Wars II.21.4). When it fell to the Roman general Titus in the Jewish struggle for independence, 6700 Jews were killed, 6000 were sent to Nero to dig the Corinthian Canal in Greece, and 30,400 were auctioned off as slaves. This occurred just decades after Jesus' death and resurrection. Although the community was rebuilt, it has been in ruins for centuries.

TIBERIAS

As you leave the tranquility of the rustic, almost idyllic, northwest shores of the Sea of Galilee, you head for the hustle and bustle of the sea's largest city—Tiberias.

Today's Tiberias is a resort town with crowded beaches and fun-loving frolickers.

It's a place of contrasts. As you enter the city, to the left you will see fishing nets drying in the Galilean sun. On the hillside to the right you will see high-rise hotels. If you follow Galilee Street, the main thoroughfare, as far as the outside of the old city wall, you can see the remains of the old rampart that encased the city. But it's filled with buses, cars and jeeps. Street urchins, tourists, bathers and bearded townspeople mingle with one another.

TIBERIAS:
A GREAT CENTER OF JUDAISM

Built sometime within the first two decades of the Christian era, TIBERIAS was the pride of Herod Antipas, son of Herod the Great. Apparently he built it over the ruins of Rakkath, an ancient town of Naphtali, and named it in honor of the Roman Emperor Tiberias.

It became the capital of Galilee under Agrippa I and the Roman procurators. After the fall of Jerusalem in A.D. 70, when the temple was destroyed, Tiberias became the great center of Judaism in the Holy Land. It was here that Rabbi Yehuda Ha'Nasi and his colleagues codified the traditional civil and ritual laws of the Jews and compiled them in the Mishnah (A.D. 200). Here, too, the Jerusalem Talmud was compiled (A.D. 400), and a system of pointing (adding vowels and punctuation to Hebrew consonants) was introduced into the Hebrew language. The great and learned men of Judaism once lived in Tiberias.

are on the southern edge of town. These thermal baths have been drawing the sick and infirm to the shores of Galilee for more than 3000 years. The hot springs contain high amounts of calcium and sulfuric salts; and for centuries they have been reported to cure rheumatism, arthritis and similar ailments. They may have been the reason for the large concentration of people around the Sea of Galilee, people who needed the healing power of Christ Jesus.

Today these hot springs range from the sublime to the ridiculous. Some resemble Turkish baths and are housed in ancient basalt buildings, complete with vaulted ceilings, domes and the mystique of the Middle Ages. Others are found in modern, sanitized clinics that resemble the spic-and-span hospitals of the United States.

Visitors to the Holy Land frequently eat lunch at restaurants that feature such hot baths. The water is incredibly warm and soothing. In the modern baths, which look just like swimming pools, it's relaxing to stand in front of the jets that propel the water into the bath directly from the underground bubbling springs. The experience is worth the small expense.

On the right is a small, unkempt park. At the water's edge, down from the artists' galleries, the teenagers of Tiberias leap into the lake from the ancient sea wall.

The only mention of Tiberias in the Bible is in John 6:23. There we read that many came from Tiberias across the sea to Capernaum, near the scene of the feeding of the 5000. But the city abounds with reminders of the New Testament era.

The world-famous hot springs of Tiberias

Near the hot springs, opposite the bus station, you will see the tomb of Rabbi Moses Ben Maimon, better known as Maimonoides. This greatest Jewish theologian of the Middle Ages was a humanist, physician, astronomer, scientist and Aristotelian philosopher. A white tomb surrounded by piles of rubble now marks the burial site of the Sephardic Jew who died in A.D. 1204.

Nearby are the tombs of Rabbi Yohanan Ben Zakkai and Rabbi Akiva. The former founded the Yavne (Yeshiva) Academy, Israel's ancient and earliest center of learning. Rabbi Akiva compiled many commentaries of the Mishnah before the Romans tortured and killed him at Caesarea in A.D. 150. The tomb of Rabbi Meir, who is known in Jewish tradition as the "Miracle Worker," is located in a white building on a hill nearly a mile south of the hot springs. This is the holiest of the tombs of Tiberias. These tombs are a constant reminder of the importance the Jews attached to this city. Tiberias is still the site of a school of rabbinic theology which has operated here for a long, long time.

Don't leave Tiberias until you've had a taste of St. Peter's fish. This local delicacy will make

your mouth water and give you no rest until you return to Tiberias for more. This white fish is a bit boney, but its succulent flavor makes up for an occasional bone. When it arrives at your table, try not to think of the fact that it's the whole fish—head, tail and all. Just lay a sprig of parsley over the fish's eye to keep him from watching as you enjoy a true Galilean feast.

A 15-minute drive south of Tiberias brings you to "six" on the Sea-of-Galilee clock. Here the Jordan River empties out of the Sea of Galilee and meanders southward toward the Dead Sea.

Just east of the Jordan is DEGANIA, Israel's oldest kibbutz. It was begun in 1909 by ten men and two women—all immigrants from the Russian town of Romni. This one-time swamp is now a showcase in modern Israel. Surrounded by plenteous orchards and gardens, fields of green vegetables and rows of golden corn, Degania is the result of determined effort and hard labor. At the entrance to the kibbutz is a Renault tank, a memorial to the farmers of Degania who stopped an advancing Syrian column with Molotov cocktails in 1948.

HAMMAT GADER

One last site along the Sea of Galilee is worth a visit. It's one of the few major attractions east of the Sea—HAMMAT GADER, also known as EL HAMMA—and it is located in the Yarmuk Valley, about 15 miles from Tiberias. You can access it via the Tiberias-Zemach road, about seven miles from the Zemach junction. The road twists and turns as it descends through a lovely ravine. To the east, beyond the barbed-wire fence—which separates Israel from Jordan—is the largest river in Jordan, the Yarmuk, which divides the Golan Heights from the Gilead Mountains.

In this area rich in vegetation are four springs—one of sweet water and three of mineral waters. The medicinal properties of these mineral springs have been lauded from antiquity. The Romans made good use of this place as a retreat or vacation spot

TIBERIAS: ISRAEL'S WINTER RESORT

Tiberias is a city with a serious past and a fun-filled present. During the winter months Israelis flock to this resort city because it offers one of the country's most pleasant winter climates. However, during the summer months the heat is oppressive; and most Israelis leave for the Mediterranean coast. A popular Israeli story is that Tiberias, down at the lake, and Safed, on top of the mountains, have the same population. Tiberias' 31,700 inhabitants live in the coolness of Safed all summer and return to Tiberias for the winter. However, not many residents of Tiberias could afford such a practice.

are those of the bath complex. Its spa rivals the great thermae of Rome and Alexandria. You can still see the remains of the spring, a small round pool, a small oval pool, a large oval pool, the Hall of Fountains, the Hall of Inscriptions and the Hall of Pillars.

A stop at Hammat Gader can accomplish three things. You can eat a nice lunch in the self-service restaurant. You can view the Roman ruins. And you can bathe in the natural open-air mineral pool. This oval-shaped pool measures approximately 60 yards by 30 yards, and its water temperature remains constant year-round at a balmy 106 degrees Fahrenheit—just like a warm bath. One more thing. You won't want to miss the adjacent alligator farm. It sports a protected walk through beautiful fields that crawl with live alligators.

Your journey around the Sea of Galilee is now complete. There is no more lovely body of water in all the world, nor is there one that holds more meaning for Christians.

because of its seclusion. So did the Jews. Here you can see a Roman amphitheater and a sixth-century synagogue with a beautiful mosaic floor. But the most remarkable ruins

The Jordan River flowing out of the Sea of Galilee

Opposite: **Beautiful flowers at Capernaum**

CHAPTER SEVEN

IN THE HEART OF THE HOLY LAND

THE WEST BANK

*"But the children of Joseph said, 'The mountain country is not enough for us'
. . . And Joshua spoke to the house of Joseph—to Ephraim and Manasseh—
saying, 'You are a great people and have great power; you shall not have one
lot only, but the mountain country shall be yours. Although it is wooded, you
shall cut it down, and its farthest extent shall be yours."*

Joshua 17:16-18

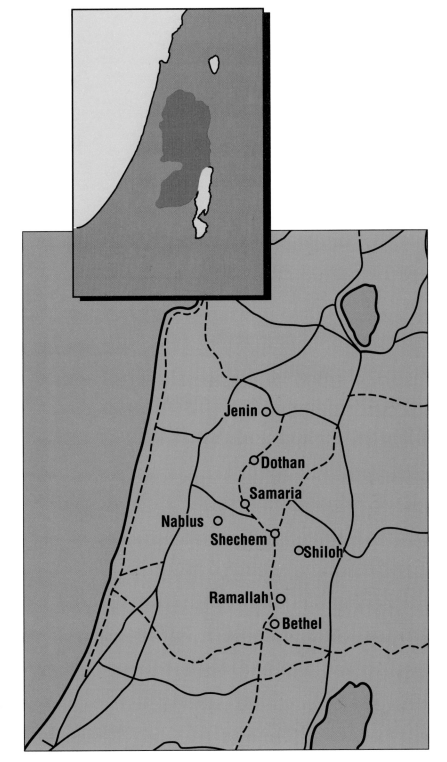

Although the Holy Land's Central Highlands extend from Mount Hermon to the Negev, the territory through which you will travel next is but a portion of that—the hill country of Ephraim and Manasseh. This is the mountainous area bordered by the coastal plain on the west and the Jordan Valley on the east. It extends from the southern edge of Esdraelon to about ten miles north of Jerusalem. Roughly speaking, this hill country, the territorial allotment to the sons of Joseph, coincides with what we have come to know as Samaria. Today it is the West Bank—the heart of the Holy Land.

In the northern sector, comprised of all of Manasseh's and most of Ephraim's territory, the mountains have valleys that run north, south and west. Rain is brought to these valleys by the Mediterranean winds. This moisture makes the Valleys of Dothan, Lebonah and others far more productive than the mountainous areas to the south. The valleys also allow free access to Samaria. As a result, new political and religious ideas have been introduced to the very center of the country.

Occasionally Christian travelers must skirt these mountain roads and passes. As political tensions rise, prudent travelers use the lower coastal roads or the valley road that parallels the Jordan River. But usually the direct route from Galilee to Jerusalem is the best, and it takes you right through the Central Highlands.

JENIN

Situated on the imaginary border between Galilee and Samaria is JENIN (En-gannim). This border is marked by the Carmel and Gilboa mountain ranges. That this is a border town is seen even in the meaning of "Jenin"—"guarded spring." The Jewish historian Josephus calls the town "Ginea" and mentions that a large number of Galileans were killed here by Samaritans as they were passing through on their way to Jerusalem (Antiq. XX.6.1).

When you enter Jenin, it will be obvious that you are passing from one territory to another, one people to another, one heritage to another. You will notice a world of difference between the Jews of Afula and the Arabs of Jenin. In fact, frequently Christian pilgrims have not been permitted to go through Jenin to the hill country. The reason is clear. At Jenin you enter the turbulent West Bank.

This area was originally part of Jordan but is now under military occupation by Israel.

Its inhabitants are mostly Arabs. Its peacekeeping forces are mostly Jews. To the Arabs it is known as "the occupied territory." To the Jews it is known as Samaria.

Jenin is mentioned in the Old Testament as En-gannim (Joshua 15:34; 19:21; 21:29). It was located, at least partially, in the territory belonging to the tribe of Issachar. But its greatest biblical importance lies in the New Testament. According to tradition, this was the city where Jesus healed the ten lepers as He passed through Samaria and Galilee (Luke 17:11-19). As you recall, only one of those healed, a Samaritan, returned to thank the Lord for His act of mercy and kindness.

As you pass through Jenin, on the road from Afula, you take a right turn at the square in the middle of the town and then proceed south through the Valley of Dothan.

DOTHAN

The Dothan Plain, a broad and fertile valley, is tucked away between the Carmel Mountains and the Gilboa Mountains. Just one mile southwest of Jenin you pass the ruins of the ancient fortress of IBLEAM. The name of this ancient town means "place of victory."

Although Ibleam was given to the tribe of Manasseh (Joshua 17:11), it could not be secured by the men of Manasseh, because the Canaanites were determined to live there (Joshua 17:12; Judges 1:27). It was near here that Jehu assassinated King Ahaziah (II Kings 9:27) and Shallum killed Israel's King

Zechariah (II Kings 15:8-10). However, as a Levitical city, Ibleam was a more peaceful town known as Bileam (I Chronicles 6:70).

As you cross the Valley of Dothan, you will see the rich red dirt of the plowed fields, a striking contrast to the chalky color of the hills. TELL DOTHAN is spread over the northeastern head of the valley, just a half mile east of the highway, some 12 miles north of Samaria.

This site is vibrant with biblical history. Joseph's brothers tended their flocks here. This was the scene of the infamous sale of Joseph by Jacob's sons to Ishmaelites journeying to Egypt (Genesis 37:13-28). Joseph's coat of many colors was torn from him here by his brothers and dipped in blood to masquerade their sin before their father (Genesis 37:23,32).

Tell Dothan is an extremely impressive mound owned and excavated by the late Joseph P. Free of Wheaton College. The surface of the mound covers a full ten acres and rises 175 feet above the plain. It is a "must see" for archaeology buffs, especially if they are photo fanatics as well. On the southern slope of the tell is a small Arab village. Most of the villagers tend sheep, just as Joseph's brothers did hundreds of years ago. Not much has changed in these fields over the years. They are still among the best grazing fields of Israel, and shepherds and their flocks abound.

Dothan is also important as the home of the Prophet Elisha (II Kings 6). It was here that he warned the king of Israel about the troop movements of the king of Syria. When the Syrian king sent "horses and chariots and a great army" (II Kings 6:14) to surround Dothan and Elisha's servant became frightened, Elisha calmed him saying, "Those who are with us are more than those who are with them" (II Kings 6:16). What follows is a fascinating story of God's grace and mercy.

SAMARIA

As you leave Tell Dothan behind, the fertile plain begins to rise to the high country of the central Holy Land. This is the hill country of Manasseh, which is lower than the hill country of Ephraim to the south.

SAMARIA: A CITY OF KINGS

Samaria was originally settled by the tribes of Ephraim and Manasseh, the children of Joseph. When the division of the Israelite kingdom came after the death of Solomon, Samaria became the capital city of the ten tribes of the north. It was the residence and the burial place of Israel's kings—Omri, Ahab, Jehu, Jehoahaz, Joash and Jehoash.

The site owes to Omri most of its importance. He bought this imposing hill from Shemer and began to build a beautiful palace on it. Six years later he died. His son Ahab continued the building project. During the continuing archaeological excavations of the site, numerous pieces of furniture with ivory overlays have been found. These validate the Bible's reference to the palace of Ahab as an "ivory house" (I Kings 22:39; Amos 3:15).

Ahab married the infamous Jezebel, who brought the worship of pagan idols to the house of Israel's king. Is it any wonder that the prophet Amos warned, "Woe to you ... who trust in the mountains of Samaria . . . who lie on beds of ivory" (Amos 6:1,4)? Jezebel induced her husband to build a temple to Baal in the city of Samaria (I Kings 16:31-33).

Although Ahab's son put away the image of Baal (II Kings 3:2), and although later Jehu destroyed Baal worship and killed the priest of Baal (II Kings 10:17-28), the damage was done. Samaria was besieged by Shalmaneser and was eventually captured and overthrown by Sargon, king of Assyria. The inhabitants were carried off into bondage in 721 B.C. (II Kings 17; 18:9-12).

But Samaria was not to be denied future existence. Later this mound was occupied by the Babylonians, Persians, Greeks and Romans. Alexander the Great besieged the city in 331 B.C., and John Hyrcanus destroyed it in 120 B.C. But the Roman general Pompey rebuilt it in 27 B.C. When Caesar Augustus gave Samaria to Herod the Great, Herod carried out large-scale renovation of the city.

SAMARIA:
PROPHETS AND PREACHERS

Throughout history many men of God have preached or prophesied in Samaria. Here Elijah destroyed the messengers of King Ahaziah and prophesied the king's death (II Kings 1). Naaman, the leper from Syria, came to Samaria to be healed by Elisha. Prophecies concerning Samaria's sin and doom frequent the pages of the Old Testament (cf. Isaiah 8:4; 9:8-21; 36:19; Jeremiah 23:13; Ezekiel 23:1-4; Hosea 7; 13:16; Amos 3:12; Micah 1:6).

Samaria had its brighter history as well. Acts 8:5,8 records, "Then Philip went down to the city of Samaria and preached Christ to them. . . . And there was great joy in that city." The Old Testament prophets had the right method—prophecy—and the right message—doom without repentance. The New Testament preachers had the right method—preaching—and the right message—"Christ died for our sins." Peter and John joined Philip at Samaria, "So when they had testified and preached the word of the Lord, they returned to Jerusalem, preaching the gospel in many villages of the Samaritans" (Acts 8:25). Today Samaria is left without such a witness to Christ's power to save men from sin.

Ahead, on the left, is a mammoth mound that is some 300 feet high, covering an unbelievable 50 acres at its summit. Sharing this mound is a unique combination of ancient and modern civilization—the hill of SAMARIA, the old capital of the northern kingdom of Israel and the present village of SEBASTE.

As you turn off the main road and climb the hill, keep a close eye out for the niches in the hillside. These are burial caves complete with ancient sarcophagi that date back to 800 B.C. They were discovered when the modern road was built.

As you approach the south side of the hill, you enter the modern Samaritan village of Sebaste. The stones of ages past have been used to build the houses of the present. These narrow, winding streets sit atop ruins of other narrow, winding streets. The houses are small; the people, poor; the lifestyle, simple.

Inside the village is a small mosque, curiously built within an old Crusader cathedral. The minaret, a tall, slender tower from which Muslims are called five times a day to prayer, dates back to the twelfth century and is an easy mark of identification. Beneath the courtyard of the mosque is a cave. The natives claim that the prophets Elisha and Obadiah are buried there.

There is a tradition that John the Baptist was imprisoned in a dungeon at this site. Machaerus, east of the Dead Sea, is a rival

claimant for this dubious honor. Nonetheless, the tradition persists that, at the very least, the head of John the Baptist was brought here by Herod Antipas at the request of Salome (Matthew 14:1-14).

Most of what you can see is from the Roman era. The fantastic colonnaded street that enters the city and the columns and ruins of the public basilica are clearly Roman. At the summit of the hill you can view a temple honoring Augustus. Samaria is one of Israel's finest exhibits of the Roman presence in a Jewish land. The forum, theater, gateway, hippodrome and street of columns give you the feeling that you are taking a stroll in ancient Rome, now crumbled and dusty. If Rome, the city of seven hills, were to have an eighth hill, Samaria would be it.

As you view the ruins, you must remember that the tragedy of Samaria is not its tumble from the heights of glory but its turning away from the heralds of God.

NABLUS

The villages of Nablus, Shechem and Sychar are like three peas in a time-warped pod, the sides of that pod being Mount Ebal and Mount Gerizim. The road from the north passes through or near these three villages, but the villages were not inhabited at the same time.

Today NABLUS/SHECHEM, with 105,000 inhabitants, is the largest town on the West Bank. Its reputation for turbulence is world-renowned. Since 1967, Nablus has spawned much of the Palestinian resistance within the territorial boundaries of Israel. Therefore, you should not linger as you pass through the town.

The white houses of Nablus, piled on the hillsides like sugar cubes, appear restful and serene. But the town itself is buzzing with activity. Here is the West Bank commercial center, also a large soap-manufacturing plant. And, in Nablus you can buy the sweetest, stickiest baklava pastries in the Holy Land.

The Roman general Titus founded the town and named it "Flavia Neopolis" in honor of his father, Flavius Vespasian. During the Greco-Roman period of history the town went by the name "Neopolis." "Nablus" is but an Arabic contraction of "Neopolis."

As you enter Nablus from the north, you will pass through a succession of smaller villages, and you will see a number of modern-looking villas. Off to your right is the Casbah, the older quarter of the town. It's charming but unsafe for visitors.

Within this quarter is an old mosque; and on the hillside above it, opposite the Muslim cemetery, is the Samaritan quarter. Here black-veiled women and white-robed men walk the streets. The men have beards and long hair and wear hats covered with red cloth. Approximately 300 Samaritans live here.

As you continue through Nablus, notice

Left: The hills of Samaria

Below: Nablus mosque

Mount Ebal and Mount Gerizim

the beautiful stained-glass windows and the blue-green dome on the mosque ahead. It's the largest mosque in this Arab town. On your left, just before you leave the town for another villa-studded suburb, you'll see the large old Arab-British prison. It is still in use.

On both sides of Nablus the landscape is dominated by mountains. To the northeast is Mount Ebal; to the southwest is Mount Gerizim. Ebal, with a height of 3077 feet, is easily recognized as the bald mountain. Gerizim, rising 2848 feet, is partially covered by trees. It was here that Israel renewed her covenants with God.

Mount Ebal was the "Mount of Cursing," while Mount Gerizim was the "Mount of Blessing" (Deuteronomy 11:29,30; 27:11-26; Joshua 8:30-34).

Joshua stationed half the tribes on Ebal and the other half on Gerizim, with the priests, Levites and the ark of the covenant in the valley between. There the people rehearsed what God's blessings would be if they were faithful and what curses would fall on them if they were not.

Joshua built an altar on Mount Ebal and "there . . . he wrote on the stones a copy of the law of Moses" (Joshua 8:30,32). And from Mount Gerizim, Jotham spoke his parable to the people of Shechem below (Judges 9:7).

Mount Gerizim is very important to the Samaritans. These people were remnants of the ten tribes who were not carried off into captivity when Samaria was captured by the Assyrians in 721 B.C. (II Kings 17:6,23). Although they were Jews, they intermarried with colonists imported to Samaria by the Assyrians in 721 B.C. (II Kings 17:24). As a result, they were a mixed race.

In their zeal for racial purity, Ezra and Nehemiah rejected Samaritan assistance in rebuilding the Temple of Jerusalem (Ezra 4:1-3). The Samaritans never forgot this rebuff. In fact, the Samaritans erected a rival temple and established a temple priesthood on Mount Gerizim.

The Samaritan woman at the well was right when she said to Jesus, "Jews have no dealings with Samaritans" (John 4:9). This woman also noted, "Our fathers worshiped on this

the mountain. They say that the 12 stones that the Israelites removed from the bed of the Jordan River, as they made their miraculous crossing (Joshua 4:1-9), are preserved in the wall of the Justinian Castle built in A.D. 583 on Gerizim's summit.

The few visitors who take the time to enter the Samaritan synagogue of upper Nablus are shown a magnificent scroll of the Pentateuch. This sect accepts only the writings of Moses as divine revelation, and their Pentateuch scrolls are some of the best preserved anywhere. The cylindrical, engraved case, carved with figures of the ark of the covenant, the menorah and the temple altar, among other things, consists of three parts, each about 18 inches long.

The treasured Torah scroll, with its green-inscribed protective wrapping, is preserved inside the case. All this is part of the worship mystique of a dying people who have staunchly maintained their uniqueness and who will be remembered by Christians as the people who gave the world the "Good Samaritan" (Luke 10:33).

SHECHEM

Biblical SHECHEM is on the main road just south of Nablus, nestled between Ebal and Gerizim. A mound, known as Tell Balata, is clearly visible off to the left. This tell has been

mountain [Mount Gerizim], and you Jews say that in Jerusalem is the place where one ought to worship" (John 4:20).

This Samaritan temple was destroyed by the Maccabean leader John Hyrcanus in 128 B.C. However, the Samaritans continue to worship on this spot today. For a week before the Passover, the whole Samaritan community leaves Nablus and camps out on top of Mount Gerizim near where the old temple stood. The entire Passover service, including the roasting of a lamb, follows the order prescribed in Exodus 12.

The Samaritans claim they have preserved altars built by Adam and Noah on the top of

STORIES FROM SHECHEM

When Abraham made his famous journey from Ur of the Chaldees to Canaan, his first stopover was Shechem. Here he built an altar to his God (Genesis 12:6,7). Later, after his 20-year hiatus in Haran, Jacob returned to Shechem and purchased a plot of the Promised Land from the sons of Hamor (Genesis 33:18-20). The rape of his daughter Dinah took place here.

Still later, his son Joseph came here in search of his brothers, only to find them in Dothan (Genesis 37:12-14). And it was to this place that the Israelites carried the bones of Joseph from Egypt for burial (Genesis 50:25; Joshua 24:32). The traditional site of Joseph's tomb is in a little white-domed house about 100 yards north of Jacob's well. Joseph's tomb is very significant for orthodox Jews. They believe that Joshua 24:32 provides documentation to show that this parcel of the Promised Land belongs to them. (The other two parcels that hold this status in their eyes are the Jerusalem Temple and the Patriarch's Tomb in Hebron.)

Shechem was one of the six cities of refuge (Joshua 20:7; 21:21). It was the scene of Joshua's farewell address to Israel, which contains his famous declaration, "As for me and my house, we will serve the LORD" (Joshua 24:15). Abimelech, the son of Gideon, attempted to establish himself as king of Israel at Shechem (Judges 9). He slew his 70 brothers and ruled in Shechem for three years before God brought judgment upon him.

Eventually Shechem did become the site of an authorized coronation. It was here that Rehoboam, son of Solomon, chose to be crowned. But Rehoboam foolishly failed to heed the advice of his father's counselors. He increased the financial burden of the Israelites. This precipitated the tax revolt led by Jeroboam and the ten northern tribes.

Shechem pops up again in the pages of the New Testament. On one of His early junkets from Judaea to Galilee, Jesus came "to a city of Samaria, which is called Sychar, near the plot of ground that Jacob gave to his son Joseph. Now Jacob's well was there" (John 4:5,6).

the site of archaeological activity off and on since 1902.

Very near Tell Balata, at the fork in the road, is the parcel of ground and the well that Jews, Samaritans, Muslims and Christians associate with Jacob's Well. You'll spot the Convent of Jacob's Well easily. Just look for the walled area to the left of it, with beautiful greenery growing inside the compound.

Once you are admitted by the Greek Orthodox monk, you enter a peaceful garden setting with beautiful flowers and well-trimmed trees and hedges. You proceed straight ahead, between two pillars, and down a path that takes you to a huge unfinished church. The Russian Orthodox Church wanted to erect a basilica that would be fitting for such a sacred spot, and they began building in 1912. Unfortunately, because of World War I, construction was halted. Today this roofless church is but a shell under which Jacob's Well is located.

Near the back of this partially weed-covered basilica are two small structures that resemble outhouses. Actually, these two enclosures are the entranceways to the 18-step passages leading down to the chapel and well. Because the traffic is one way, you'll enter the left enclosure. The stairs are steep and nar-

Jacob's Well

row. The room in which the well is located has painted tiles on the floor and paintings and icons on the wall. However, the first thing you'll notice are the many shiny incense burners hanging from the ceiling.

The well is in the center of the room. The lone, gracious monk will lower a metal pail into the well (which is 115 feet deep) to get you a drink. The pail travels 90 feet before it reaches the water. Although you can't see the water, it's fun to lean over the center of the seven-and-one-half-foot-wide, three-foot-high well covering and peer down the shaft. When the monk reels back the pail filled with water, he will offer you a drink in a tin cup. Although the water is crystal clear, great tasting and frosty cold, remember that every other pilgrim to visit this site drank out of that same tin cup. You may want to have your own collapsible cup ready, just in case.

SHILOH

As you head south through the territory of Manasseh, you pass biblical OPHRAH on your left. This Benjamite town (Judges 6:11-24) is where the angel of the LORD appeared to Gideon and called him to service for God. After the angel proved he was indeed the messenger of Jehovah, Gideon exclaimed, "I have seen the Angel of the LORD face to face" (Judges 6:22). Here he built an altar to the Lord, calling it Jehovah-shalom, "The Lord our Peace" (verse 24). Gideon was buried in

Greek Orthodox priest drawing water from Jacob's Well

Ophrah (Judges 8:32).

In a few more minutes, you will pass the village of LUBBAN and leave the beautiful Lebonah Valley. In biblical days this area was famous for myrrh and other incense. Today myrrh is still grown in the valley, along with a more modern commodity—tobacco. This area marks the traditional frontier between Samaria and Judaea.

Up ahead, as you climb out of the valley to higher terrain, you will be able to see two nearly perfect stone watchtowers on your left. They are circular with wide bottoms tapering slightly toward the top, and they are made entirely of stones gleaned from the fields round about. They are just tall enough to get a shepherd out of the reach of hungry animals, and they are useful in guarding the road against intruders. These watchtowers are worth photographing. Watchtowers are prominently featured in the Bible (Isaiah 5:2; Matthew 21:33-44).

Soon you will see a five-foot stone pillar pointing to SHILOH. The ruins are located on the spur road that cuts back on the left toward Ophrah. At Shiloh you can see the remains of a group of ancient tombs cut in

the rock, as well as small piles of stones and two blazing white but unfinished and roofless churches. These were begun in the 1930's on the site of ruined Byzantine churches.

BETHEL

As you leave Shiloh, the road twists and turns southward through hills blanketed with olive groves. You have now passed into the hill country of Ephraim, and the inclines become steeper. Eleven miles north of Jerusalem you arrive at biblical BETHEL. About a mile and a half off the main road to the east is BEITIN, the Arab village adjacent to the site of Bethel.

Bethel was originally called "Luz" (Genesis 28:19). Abraham built his second altar on this site upon arriving from Ur of the Chaldees (Genesis 12:8). After returning from Egypt to escape the Canaanite famine (Genesis 13:3,4), Abraham again migrated here. Later, strife between his and Lot's herdsmen forced a painful separation (Genesis 13:5-12).

Bethel gains its true prominence, however, because of Abraham's grandson. After fleeing from the wrath of his duped brother Esau, Jacob spent the night at Bethel (Genesis 28:11-22), where he saw the vision of a ladder with angels ascending and descending from heaven. Jacob's response to this dream was, "How awesome is this place! This is none other than the house of God, and this is the gate of heaven!" (Genesis 28:17). Hence, the name "Luz" was changed to "Bethel" ("House of God"). Jacob revisited Bethel after he returned from his sojourn in Haran (Genesis 35:1-8).

After Israel captured this royal Canaanite city (Joshua 12:16; Judges 1:22-26), Bethel became a major religious center in Israelite life. The city was on Samuel's circuit as prophet and judge (I Samuel 7:16).

When the ten northern tribes seceded from Judah, Jeroboam set up two golden-calf worship centers in the north to keep the tribes from making the pilgrimage to Jerusalem to worship. Dan was the northernmost site; Bethel the southernmost.

SHILOH: A LESSON IN JUDGMENT

Today there is precious little to indicate that Shiloh was once the pride of Israel and her first capital for 300 years prior to the conquest of Jerusalem.

Here the tribes assembled to receive their allotments of the Promised Land (Joshua 18-22). The ark of the covenant found a home here and the tabernacle was erected (Joshua 18:1; Judges 18:31). This was the center of Israel's religion. Eli, the high priest, judged Israel from here, and Hannah came here to pray that God would give her a son (I Samuel 1:1-10). When Samuel was born, Hannah brought him to be raised in the service of the Lord (I Samuel 1:1-28). Eli died at Shiloh (I Samuel 4) and Samuel judged Israel in his place (I Samuel 7:16,17).

About 1050 B.C., Shiloh was destroyed by the Philistines. They took possession of the ark of the covenant, and the once sacred city was left in ruins. After that time, Shiloh's ruins became a point of reference and comparison in God's repeated warnings to His people (Psalm 78:59-61). The Prophet Jeremiah used Shiloh as an example of the destruction God would bring on Jerusalem if Israel did not repent (Jeremiah 7:12-15; 26:6,7). Israel refused to repent, and Jerusalem experienced a destruction similar to that of Shiloh (II Kings 25:8-11). God always provides opportunity for repentance; but when there is no repentance, God always keeps His word.

Later when King Jeroboam burned incense at Bethel, he was denounced by an unnamed prophet (I Kings 12:33; 13:2). The prophet predicted that Josiah would offer the bones of the priests on that altar. During King Josiah's reforms of the sixth century, he removed bones from nearby tombs and burned them on the altar, fulfilling this prophecy exactly (II Kings 23:15-19).

Because he foretold King Jeroboam's death, the prophet Amos was forbidden to prophesy in Bethel and was expelled from the city. This religious center was frequently the subject of Amos' prophecies (Amos 3:14; 4:4; 5:5; 7:10, 13), as well as Jeremiah's (Jeremiah 48:13). Bethel fell with Samaria in 721 B.C. when the Assyrians swept through the land.

As you visit the ancient site of Bethel, you will be in much less awe than Jacob was on his first visit there. The archaeological finds have not been earthshaking, and the excavations have been partially restored to use by the residents of Beitin. Nevertheless, the air on this hill is vibrant with history, and the stones beneath your feet—and there are millions of them—are rounded by the feet of ancient Israelite worshipers at the site that once was the "House of God."

RAMALLAH

The road to Ramallah winds through a rustic landscape—vineyards, vegetable fields and numerous small villages. Just eight miles north of Jerusalem, Ramallah is one of the most popular resorts in the Holy Land. The name in Arabic means "the Heights of the Lord." The town's elevation, at 2930 feet above sea level (300 feet higher than Jerusalem), brings it cool weather when much of Israel is warm and sultry. Until the June War of 1967 Ramallah was the best summer resort in Jordan. It was popularly called the "Switzerland of Jordan." It is now part of the West Bank—occupied territory.

Now the largest village between Jerusalem and Nablus, Ramallah has 26,000 inhabitants. It is surprising to learn that 25 percent are U.S. citizens. But don't let this fool you. Although it is an educational and commercial center, Ramallah is decidedly an Arab town. The veiled women and the water-pipe-smoking men provide much local color. Almost the entire Arab population is Christian. Since no biblical significance is attached to Ramallah, most twentieth-century Christian crusaders to the Holy Land drive right by this neat and clean city. But should you take the time to zip up to Ramallah from Jerusalem, you'll enjoy the green hillsides, the plush villas and the town's beautiful park. Also, the former palace of King Hussein is located here. Don't expect to see an opulent wonder. It is plain and unostentatious.

Perhaps the best reason to visit Ramallah is to buy the Arab pastries. Here you can treat your sweet tooth to baklava as thin as can be and covered with honey, coconut or pistachio nuts. It's a taste delight from the hill country of the Holy Land that you'll never forget.

AN INTRIGUING RIVER

THE JORDAN VALLEY

"It came to pass in those days that Jesus came from Nazareth of Galilee, and was baptized by John in the Jordan. And immediately, coming up from the water, He saw the heavens parting and the Spirit descending upon Him like a dove. Then a voice came from heaven, 'You are my beloved Son, in whom I am well pleased.' And immediately the Spirit drove Him into the wilderness."

Mark 1:9-12

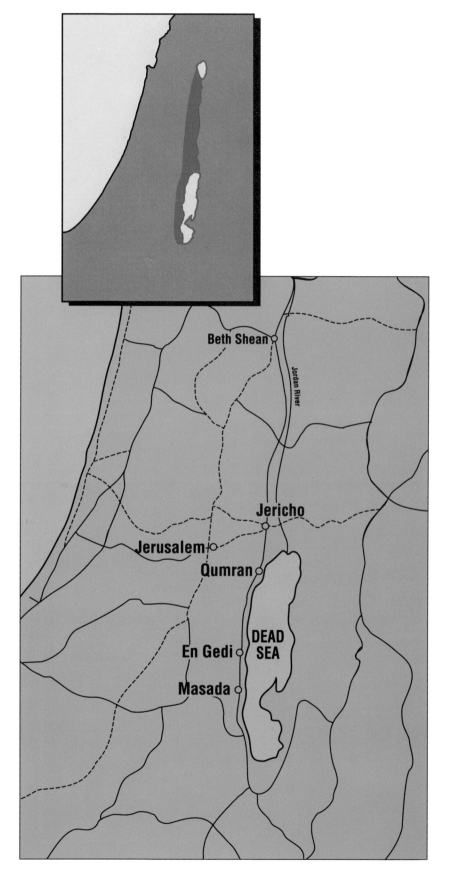

The Jordan Valley is much more than a valley; it is a deep depression in the ground. The valley is referred to as the Rift Valley because it is the site of one of the world's greatest geological faults. This rift begins far in the north between the Lebanon and Anti-Lebanon Mountains and cuts a path southward. It deepens steadily until it reaches the Dead Sea and then rises slightly until it reaches the Gulf of Aqabah and the Red Sea.

This great valley is divided naturally into three parts: the upper Jordan or Hula basin; the middle Jordan or Tiberias district; and the lower Jordan, affectionately known to the Arabs as the "Ghor." The land closest to the mountains on both sides of the river is developed, with groves of bananas and lush fields of vegetables. The subtropical climate contributes to the valley's ability to produce juicy fruits and gigantic vegetables. Closer to the river itself sand has blown over the years, forming barren mounds where nothing can grow. Then just next to the water's edge there is another depression in the ground, a mini-rift, known as the "Zor." Down in this trench is the Jordan River. The banks of the Jordan are dark green with trees and brush,

three times have its waters been stopped by the miraculous power of God. The first was when the Israelites entered the Promised Land while the river was in its flood stage (Joshua 3:13-17; 4:18). The second was when Elijah struck the waters to allow him and Elisha to cross over (II Kings 2:6-8). The third was when Elisha returned to Canaan after Elijah's translation (II Kings 2:12-15). Elisha caused the axe head to float on these same waters (II Kings 6:4-7).

While the floor of the Rift Valley is dominated by the winding river, there are several very important cities in the valley as well. Add the cities along the western shore of the Dead Sea to your planned trip and you will have an exciting adventure.

Two main roads lead to the Jordan Valley from the north. One stretches almost due south from the tip of the Sea of Galilee at DEGANIA leading toward Beth Shean. Nine miles south of the sea the road passes BELVOIR, which is on the right. A National Parks Authority city, Belvoir offers an excellent view of the Jordan Valley. The remains of a twelfth-century French Crusader fortress can be seen here as well. The second road to the valley approaches from the northwest. It begins at Afula in the Jezreel Valley and ends at Beth Shean.

If you take this latter route, from Afula, you will cross the valley and soon pass the Kibbutz JEZREEL (or Yizreel). The modern town was founded in 1949, near the ancient site of Jezreel. This was the city to which Elijah ran after defeating the prophets of Baal (I Kings 18:42-46). King Ahab built one of his palaces here. An innocent man named Naboth had a vineyard next to this palace (I Kings 21:1). And Jezebel, Ahab's wicked queen, arranged for his murder. This did not go unnoticed by God. Elijah prophesied that Jezebel would be eaten by dogs and Ahab's blood would be licked up by dogs. Both prophecies were fulfilled (I Kings 21:17-25; 22:37,38; II Kings 9:30-37). Jehu's judgments on the house of Ahab occurred in and around Jezreel (II Kings 9:14-37; 10:6-11).

a striking contrast to the brown, barren sand just a few feet away.

The Jordan springs from the foothills of Mount Hermon and flows down to the Hula Valley, through the Sea of Galilee and down the Jordan Valley to the Dead Sea. It's the largest of Israel's seven permanent rivers, and it's the only one that does not flow into the Mediterranean. Jordan's headlong drop from its source has given it the name "Yarden," meaning the "downrusher" or "descender." It's the only river in the world that flows predominantly below sea level.

Along its 158-mile course from north to south the Jordan descends more than 2300 feet. But its path is uncertain, meandering over much of the Ghor, winding about 200 miles from the Sea of Galilee to the Dead Sea—a distance of only 65 miles. The river overflows its banks during the rainy season, but most of the year it is just a small muddy stream with a swift current.

While it doesn't compare with the width of the Amazon, the length of the Nile or the might of the Mississippi, the Jordan has figured prominently in history. No less than

Near Kibbutz Jezreel and just off the main road is EIN HAROD, a copious spring that emerges from the foot of Mount Gilboa. This is where God reduced Gideon's army to 300 men. He instructed Gideon to bring his men to the water to observe how they drank: "Everyone who laps from the water with his tongue, as a dog laps, you shall set apart by himself. . . . Then the LORD said to Gideon, 'By the three hundred men who lapped I will save you'" (Judges 7:5-7). Today this site is under the administration of the National Parks Authority. It includes a modern youth hostel, a culture hall and an amphitheater, as well as a developed community.

Just a short distance beyond Ein Harod, on the road to the Jordan Valley, there is a highway sign for BEIT ALPHA. This communal settlement is off the main road but boasts a most interesting archaeological discovery. In 1922, Polish pioneers settled this area, and during the process of draining a nearby swamp, they discovered the remnant of an old synagogue.

The mosaic floor is amazing. Divided into three panels, the mosaic depicts Abraham's

BETH SHEAN IN BIBLICAL HISTORY

Although Beth Shean was part of the inheritance of Manasseh (Joshua 17:11), this tribe was never able to expel the Canaanites (Judges 1:27) because of the Canaanite chariots of iron (Joshua 17:16). Perhaps the city's greatest claim to fame is its association with the death of King Saul. Nearby, at Mount Gilboa, Israel's first king and his sons were killed by the Philistines. As was the custom of these "Sea People," the Philistines carried the bodies of Saul and his sons and fastened them to the city wall of Beth Shean. They would have remained there in ignominy had not the brave men of Jabesh Gilead retrieved the bodies by night and buried them (I Samuel 31:8-13). Later David exhumed the bodies and reburied them in the hill country of Benjamin (II Samuel 21:12-14).

sacrifice of Isaac (Genesis 22:3-13), a Zodiac wheel and a number of religious emblems such as the ark and the menorah. An Aramaic inscription refers to Emperor Justinus (A.D. 518-527) as the ruler when the mosaic was laid.

BETH SHEAN

The next stop will be BETH SHEAN. The valley has been steadily descending, and after it passes below sea level, its floor plummets. You have left the Esdraelon Valley and are now nearing the eastern end of the Jezreel Valley. (Technically they are not the same, although few draw the distinction.) Jezreel rapidly drops to meet the Jordan Valley. They merge at Beth Shean, also spelled "Beit She'an" and "Bethshan."

This site bears remarkable similarities to Megiddo. Both are situated at a strategic pass—one on each end of Israel's only east-west valley. Both have witnessed a continual parade of armies marching to and from battle. Both have fine archaeological specimens featuring multiple levels of occupation. Both

Left: The ruins of Beth Shean

housed garrisons for Solomon's mighty armies (I Kings 4:12). Other similarities abound.

As you travel, you will notice the rise in temperature that accompanies the drop in elevation. At Beth Shean, where you enter the Jordan Valley, you're already 300 feet below sea level. The fields are quite productive, even though this area receives only 12 inches of rainfall annually. Fertile fields lie to the east of the modern city. They are watered by streams flowing down from Mount Gilboa. You can easily recognize the crops growing here—wheat, cotton and bananas, as well as a wide variety of vegetables.

The ancient mound at Beth Shean is one of the most important archaeological tells in Israel. Between 1921 and 1933, Beth Shean was excavated by a team from the University of Pennsylvania. No less than 18 strata of civilization, going back to 3000 B.C., have been identified. Because of Beth Shean's ideal location, its fertile fields and abundant streams, each new group of settlers would simply repopulate the site rather than locate a new site. Consequently, the city is like an 18-layer cake. The lower the layer, the older would be the occupation.

Levels nine through seven coincide with the Egyptian occupation of the site. Egyptian artifacts abound, including sarcophagi, scarabs and a stele of Pharaoh Seti I (1303 B.C.). Strata four and five, the Israelite level, contain many interesting Hebrew ceramics, characteristic of King Saul's day. Closer to the top, evidences of the Greek era (when the city was renamed Scythopolis), the Roman era and the Byzantine era have been discovered. The uppermost level contains jugs and farm implements from the Arab and Turkish settlers on the site. Beth Shean is a living lesson in archaeology.

If you have the stamina, you may want to climb the mound to the top. It is an impressive site, and climbing it is an impressive feat. While the top of the tell is flat, the sides slope upward at a 45 degree angle. All along the way you will spot pieces of broken pottery, ceramics, jug chips and other items—all from recent decades. The real artifacts of Beth Shean are in the Rockefeller Museum in Jerusalem and the University of Pennsylvania Museum in Philadelphia.

Near the Tell Beth Shean you can see Palestine's most perfectly preserved Roman theater. Strikingly similar to the Roman theater at Caesarea, this marvel consists of 15 white limestone tiers in near perfect condition with several additional tiers of black basalt in deteriorating condition. The upper gallery, with its nine exit tunnels, makes the Beth Shean theater resemble the Los Angeles Coliseum.

The Roman theater at Beth Shean

This theater was built in A.D. 200; and it is estimated that it seated 8000 spectators.

Few sites in the Holy Land dominate the surrounding countryside like Beth Shean. Few sites preserve the archaeological integrity of a mound like Beth Shean. Few sites have been a fortress for the Canaanites, Egyptians, Philistines, Israelites, Greeks, Maccabeans, Romans, Byzantines, Turks, British and Israelis like Beth Shean. Modern Beth Shean, with its 13,100 inhabitants, is quiet now.

The journey south through the Jordan Valley to Jericho is long. As you drive, keep an eye on the black-green vegetation to your left. Although you can't see the water, as long as you see that black-green strip alongside, you know that the Jordan River is there. To your right is the sandy barrenness of the upper Jordan Valley, and beyond that you can see the green of its hills.

ROADS TO JERICHO

There are four approaches to Jericho—one from each point of the compass. From the south the road from the Dead Sea twists and turns north, then west, then north again. From the east, the road is straight, coming from the Jordan River and the single crossing point from Jordan into Israel, the Allenby Bridge. The five-and-one-half-mile trip can take hours because of the government red tape on both sides and because of the Israeli border check on the west side of the river.

This bridge is near the location where the Israelites crossed the river and entered the Promised Land. For those ancient Israelites traveling westward, the knowledge that Jericho was dead ahead brought little comfort. For today's traveler crossing the Allenby westward, that same knowledge may be the only source of comfort after demoralizing detainment and delays.

The third, and by far the most famous, approach to Jericho is the legendary Jericho Road. Three such roads have existed, crossing from the northern end of the Dead Sea and ascending to the northern boundary of Judaea. One road was built by the Romans and was traveled by our Lord Jesus many times. A second road was built during the British Mandate (1918-1948) and curved around the hills of this eastern wilderness. The present road was built in the early 1960's and is a very good highway, well paved and wide—for a road in the Middle East. It is well contoured to the wild and rugged terrain. Where it carves passes in the mountains, it exposes crusty stone.

Above left: The old Roman road to Jericho

Below: The wilderness between Jericho and Jerusalem

FROM JERUSALEM: THE ROAD DOWN TO JERICHO

If you glance at a map of the Holy Land, you might think the word "down" is ill-chosen. Jericho is actually 17 miles to the northeast of Jerusalem. Ordinarily we would describe that as going "up" to Jericho. But here's where knowledge of the topography of the Holy Land comes in handy.

Jerusalem is approximately 2700 feet above sea level. The floor of the Jordan Valley at the Dead Sea is 1320 feet below sea level, depending on the season. Jericho itself is 850 feet below sea level. Hence the 45-minute drive from Jerusalem to Jericho means a drop in elevation of nearly 3600 feet. It's an ear-popping experience. And the road is definitely *down* to Jericho.

Judaea stretches in front of you. The word "wilderness" refers to absolute desolation, similar to that of the badlands of South Dakota.

This wilderness is far less habitable than the sand of the Negev, and it is virtually without rain and therefore without vegetation. It is a place of solitude and refuge, as witnessed to by David, Herod and Jesus. It looks like a lifeless moonscape—but don't confuse the absence of civilization with the absence of life. As you descend on the Jericho Road, you will pass black-clad Bedouin women, their friendly, waving children and their tiny herds of sheep. Rarely are the Bedouin men seen, but their black tent-houses, erected on stakes on distant hills or nestled in ravines, stand out in bold contrast to the chalky sands of the wilderness.

The Bedouin live a simple life-style in floorless black tents. Their faces are dirt-covered and their dilapidated shoes are decades old. However, if you look closely, you will see a tractor or a car—usually a Mercedes Benz—behind the black tent. A television antenna is attached to the roof of the tent. Perhaps they view "Days of Our Lives" during the Arabian nights.

Only a few miles out of Jerusalem you will spot on the right-hand side an old khan or caravansary. (A khan is an ancient stopover where travelers could find accommodations for themselves and their camels.) This is the

When the stone is in the shadows, a variety of pastel colors is revealed. When the mountain sun strikes the stone, orange and rose colors predominate. Alongside this highway you can still see the traces of the British road and occasionally the old Roman road.

Shortly after you leave Jerusalem on the Jericho Road and pass Bethany, you come to a knoll. At that point the great wilderness of

Right: **The Good Samaritan Inn**

traditional INN OF THE GOOD SAMARITAN. As you look at the millions of crags and crannies from which robbers could prey on unsuspecting travelers, you can see the appropriateness of the Lord's story about the Good Samaritan and the man who "went down from Jerusalem to Jericho, and fell among thieves" (Luke 10:30).

The present inn was built by the Turks nearly 400 years ago. It has been renovated and made into a rest-room stop, a gift shop and a museum. It is impossible to determine whether this was the spot where the "neighbor" lay robbed and bleeding. However, at one time this was an important landmark. Prior to the June War of 1967, the Jordanian police used this ancient building as a patrol station from which they monitored the activities of the wilderness. Today it is but a brief stop between Jericho and Jerusalem.

Frequently you can see a black Bedouin tent adjacent to the inn. The friendly owner will invite you into his tent and brew some coffee or tea for you. He will play his single-stringed Bedouin "guitar" and even sing a few tunes. It is an interesting experience and well worth a visit. Outside, the Bedouin's camel awaits your ascent for an all-too-short but deliriously fun ride.

A bit farther down the road you pass a highway marker on your right. It is the five-foot-tall masonry monument indicating in Arabic, Hebrew and English that you have passed below

sea level. At this point, both Arab and Jewish guides usually quip, "You'd better roll up your windows or you'll get wet." Respond with a polite chuckle so as not to encourage them. Their jokes can get much worse.

The most interesting way to descend to Jericho is to leave the modern road and travel the windy but much more interesting old Roman road. Watch for the sign for Wadi Qelt, also spelled "Wadi Kelt." Turn left, make a quick right and you're on your way. Along the way, keep your eyes peeled for shepherds and herds of sheep. The Bedouin love to bring their herds to graze in this wilderness.

Soon you'll come to a rise where you can park and walk a few hundred feet to the crest of the hill. There you may gasp, for you'll be looking over the lip, deep into the gorge of WADI QELT. Down in the gorge, precariously perched on a ledge on the other side, is the Greek Orthodox MONASTERY OF ST. GEORGE. Built near the site where Elijah the prophet was fed by the ravens, it is breathtakingly beautiful, with its sparkling white domes against the rock cliff. Tiny caves pockmark the cliff. These are used as cells by the reclusive monks during days when they isolate themselves in prayer. The monastery was completely destroyed by the Persians and was later rebuilt. It is a monument to the resilience of the monks.

Above: Bedouin shepherds with their sheep

Left: Bedouin tent

As you approach Jericho, you will round a bend and will see the verdant plain. The city of palm trees is centered against a tapestry of colors. On your right you will pass some buildings and one of the largest, most brilliant poinciana trees you will ever see. On your left, you will see the ruins of HEROD'S WINTER PALACE. Herod built this winter playground near the mouth of the Wadi Qelt, a rainy-season stream. He died here in 4 B.C.

JERICHO

If you take the Jordan Valley road south from Beth Shean to Jericho, you'll pass CALIPH HISHAM'S PALACE on the left, just before you get to the city. This palace was a winter resort for the Omayyad caliphs whose capital was in Damascus, Syria. Hisham's Palace was beautiful, rivaling or exceeding the beauty of Herod's winter palace. Although it was destroyed by an earthquake in A.D. 747, its intricate heating systems, bath houses, saunas and pools have been preserved. The elegant buildings are now part of the National Parks Authority. Many of the palace's artifacts have been removed to the Palestine Archaeological Museum in Jerusalem.

There are two "must sees" here. One is the incredible stone window in the center courtyard of the ruins. It is one of the most photographed structures in Bible country. The second is the magnificent mosaic floor of the bath. This mosaic contains beautiful wilderness scenes of gazelles feeding under a pomegranate tree, one of which is being attacked by a lion. It is the most amazing mosaic in this part of the world.

Hisham's Palace, also known as "Khirbet el Mafjar," is not included on many tours to the Holy Land; but it is certainly worth the stop.

Talking about JERICHO can be confusing.

THE CURSE OF JERICHO

Perhaps Old Jericho will be a disappointment to you. The mound is large but archaeologically unimpressive. That's because you don't see the fabled walls of Jericho. Moreover, many seasons of excavation have disturbed the site, and the feet of millions of tourists have pounded the mound into submission. But never forget the importance of the 23 different levels of occupation upon which you stand.

This walled city (Joshua 6:1) was once the front line of defense for the ancient Canaanites. If Israel was to claim her promised possession, Jericho must fall. Joshua sent in the spies to survey the city's strength (Joshua 2:1-15). His greatest fears were confirmed. Jericho was impregnable. It was only by the power of Jehovah, the Lord God of Israel, that the walls came tumbling down and the city was subdued (Joshua 6:13-17).

Joshua pronounced a curse on anyone who would attempt to rebuild Jericho (Joshua 6:26): "Cursed be the man before the LORD who rises up and builds this city Jericho; he shall lay its foundation with his firstborn, and with his youngest he shall set up its gates." In spite of this curse, Hiel the Bethelite rebuilt the city. First Kings 16:34 records, "In his days Hiel the Bethelite built Jericho. He laid its foundation with Abiram his firstborn, and with his youngest son Segub he set up its gates, according to the word of the LORD, which He had spoken through Joshua the son of Nun." God always keeps His word.

I have an Arab friend whose father once served as mayor of Jericho. He told me that the local families believe that an inordinate number of first male children of Jericho families die even today. My friend's parents lost their firstborn son. The families of Jericho are fully aware of Joshua's curse.

There are actually three "Jerichos." The first is Old Jericho, the Old Testament Jericho (Tell el Sultan), near Elisha's Fountain. The second is New Jericho, the modern city peppered with palm trees. And the third is the New Testament Jericho, to the south and west of the other sites, near the Wadi Kelt and Herod's winter palace.

As you approach the city from Beth Shean and the north, your first stop is Old Jericho (Tell el Sultan). You know you're close when you pass what looks like flat-roofed adobe huts abandoned by a fleeing tribe of North American Indians. Actually, this ghost town is one of two refugee camps, the largest such camps built in Jordan at the time of the 1948 war. (The other is south of town.) When the Israeli armies moved into this sector in 1967, the refugees fled; and the houses now stand in eerie silence.

About a minute later, you'll arrive at the Old Testament Jericho. This large mound, 1200 feet long and 50 feet high, is surrounded by a security fence. You'll enter near Elisha's Fountain and immediately you begin to climb up and to your right. A succession of archaeological seasons was undertaken here by John Garstang and later by Kathleen Kenyon. The circular stone Canaanite tower, the ancient walls and the gates with arches are especially interesting. You have to look down into the mound to see them.

From the top of this mound you get a perfect view of the MOUNT OF TEMPTATION. With your back to Jericho, look toward the

Above: **Mount of Temptation**

spring originates under the mound of Old Jericho, and it waters the entire area. In the Old Testament, Jericho is known as the "city of palm trees" (Deuteronomy 34:3). Palm trees also abound today. The streets are lined with date palms and flamboyant-red flowering poinciana trees. You would not expect to see such a beautiful oasis in such an arid valley. But the secret of Jericho's green in a sea of brown is Elisha's abundant stream.

The water is crystal clear and cool as it bubbles out of the ground and then runs through the channel along the street. You can dip your hands into it and feel the swiftness of the current.

But the water wasn't like that years ago, when Elijah and Elisha and the "sons of the prophets" were at Jericho (II Kings 2:4-18). At that time the two great prophets miraculously crossed the Jordan; and after the mantle was transferred from Elijah to Elisha, Elisha returned to Jericho. Here he found this stream to be polluted and of no value to the city. He

ridge of mountains across the valley. Near the top of this ridge you will notice a line of buildings similar in appearance to the cliff dwellings at Mesa Verde in the American West. This is the GREEK MONASTERY OF THE FORTY DAYS, believed to be the site of the second of Jesus' three temptations by Satan. After fasting for 40 days, Jesus was taken by the Devil "up on a high mountain" (Luke 4:1-13). In these same mountains the Israelite spies hid for three days while the king of Jericho pursued them toward the Jordan River.

After you leave the mound of Jericho (be careful of the slippery steps on your way down), stop across the street at either the OLD JERICHO REST HOUSE or THE MOUNT OF TEMPTATION RESTAURANT. Jericho is hot about ten months a year. At one of these Jericho rest houses, you can eat some lunch or buy a cold soft drink. Another good way to cool off is to buy some delicious Jericho fruit. Bananas, oranges, dates, pistachio nuts and a variety of melons await you.

Right: **The Jericho pumphouse sends the waters of Elisha's Fountain throughout the city.**

Up the street to the north a few hundred feet you will see ELISHA'S FOUNTAIN. The

cast a handful of salt into the water and by the power of the LORD the stream was "healed"; and until this day it has remained pure (vv. 19-22). Now this copious fountain is the lifestream of the city.

Thought to be the oldest, continuously inhabited city in the world, Jericho has played a major role in the history of the Holy Land. Of course, Joshua and the Israelites fought the famous battle here. In addition, the messengers of King David tarried at Jericho until the indignities they received at the hands of the princes of Ammon were removed (II Samuel 10:1-5). And it was near Jericho that King Zedekiah was captured by the Chaldeans (II Kings 25:5-7; Jeremiah 39:5-7; 52:8-11).

Jericho was also prominent in the New Testament era. It was here that Zacchaeus, the short, little man, climbed a sycamore tree to see Jesus (Luke 19:1-10). (Two such ancient trees still exist in the town today—one at the Greek Orthodox Church and the other on the right as you enter Jericho from the Allenby Bridge.) Great multitudes followed Jesus from Jericho on His way to the triumphal entry into Jerusalem. It was on this occasion that blind Bartimaeus was healed (Mark 10:46-52).

Knowing that there was more than one town of Jericho helps clear up an alleged discrepancy in the Bible. Matthew records that Bartimaeus was healed, "as [Jesus and His disciples] departed from Jericho" (Matthew 20:29). Luke records that the healing took place "as [Jesus] was come near Jericho" (Luke

LUNCH AT JERICHO

Lunching in Jericho is an unforgettable experience. Around the town square, which is lined with shops selling fresh fruits and vegetables, soaps, sacks of dried tobacco and just about everything else, you can pick up a snack. But the real atmosphere of a lunch in Jericho is savored only by eating in one of the city's garden restaurants.

On Ein el Sultan Street, for example, there are a number of such restaurants. The food is very good and inexpensive. The most popular dish is chicken served with carrots, peas and pita bread, along with several bowls of various pastes into which you dip your pita. The flavors of these pastes or sauces are indescribable, but you owe it to yourself to try them all.

One word of caution. Every lunch in Jericho is accompanied by an army of flies. I think they followed the Israelites from Egypt. These restaurants ought to be called "Shoo and Chew." One other thing. Don't be shocked to see a cat climb right up on a table that hasn't been cleared and eat what patrons have left behind. This is socially acceptable in Jericho and, in fact, in most Arab cities. But the cats will await their turn, so enjoy lunch. Bon appetit.

18:35). The simple explanation for this is that both writers were right. The healing of Bartimaeus probably took place on the road leaving one Jericho and coming near the other. The Bible stands.

As you leave the beautiful oasis of Jericho and make your way south to the Dead Sea, once again you will see the black-green streak that identifies the plant growth of the Zor, the lowest trench of the valley through which the Jordan River flows.

It was near here, at BETHABARA, that John the Baptist baptized Jesus (Mark 1:1-11); but you cannot approach the river at this point because you would have to enter a military zone to do so. But perhaps you can make out the Abyssinian-styled MONASTERY OF JOHN

The southern part of the Dead Sea near Zoar

the lowest spot on earth.

Some spots on the floor of the Dead Sea are approximately 2600 feet below sea level, as far beneath the surface as the surface is beneath sea level.

The Dead Sea is incredible. While the ocean's concentration of salt is only 5-7 percent, the Dead Sea's concentration of salt and other minerals is approximately 33 percent at the northern end and 50 percent at the southern end. Even the Great Salt Lake in Utah can't hold a candle to this.

The waters are so dense, so buoyant, it's impossible to sink. Literally, you can sit up in the water as if you were in a chair. You don't have to be an Olympic swimmer to swim here. You can't fail. But if you should swim in the Dead Sea, do not open your eyes or mouth. In fact, every little cut or shaving nick will smart from the salt in the water, but it will heal rapidly.

Once you leave the sea, you must shower

THE BAPTIST, built on this spot.

THE DEAD SEA

Below: Dead Sea swimmers

Right: Qumran, Cave 4, where some Dead Sea Scrolls were found

Next, drive south along the western shore of the DEAD SEA. The great geological fault, or crack in the earth, you've been following down the Jordan Valley now reaches its lowest point. You've arrived at the Dead Sea, approximately 1320 feet below sea level—

A MODERN TRAGEDY

For centuries the Dead Sea was 47 miles long and about 11 miles wide, covering approximately 394 square miles. Historically about one billion cubic feet of water flowed each year into the sea, mainly from the Jordan River.

You might expect that, since there is no outlet to the sea, the water level would be constantly rising, but it hasn't. For centuries a delicate balance was maintained between intake and daily evaporation caused by the intense heat and dryness of the Jordan Valley. But all that has changed.

I always thought the Dead Sea, as depicted on Bible Lands maps, looked like an inverted fetal mouse facing south, with the Jordan River as a long, squiggly tail. This was because a peninsula jutted out from the eastern shore into the sea about a third of the way from the southern end. This was called the "Lisan Peninsula" or "The Tongue."

But today the Dead Sea is actually two seas, split by the high ground of the sea bottom at "The Tongue" and connected with each other by a water channel. While the northern portion remains about 1250 feet deep on the average, the southern portion is comprised of a series of artificial pools; and it averages only 16-20 feet deep.

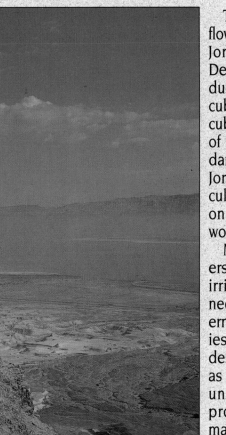

The amount of water flowing annually from the Jordan River into the Dead Sea has been reduced from one billion cubic feet to 300 million cubic feet. The pumping of water out of the Jordan River by Israel and Jordan for use in agriculture has taken its toll on one of God's great wonders.

Many Israelis and others feel that, while the irrigation projects are necessary for the modern agricultural economies of Israel and Jordan, destroying a unique sea as old as time itself is unthinkable. Several proposals have been made to save the Dead Sea, and perhaps the most interesting one was the Med-Dead Canal. First proposed in 1944 by the American geophysicist Walter C. Lowdermilk, this plan called for a canal to be dug from the Mediterranean Sea to the Dead Sea. The flow of the salty ocean water to the salty sea water would be controlled, and, because of the tremendous 1300-foot drop from the Mediterranean to the Dead Sea (eight times the fall at Niagara), an astounding amount of electricity could be generated. But the project seemed too gargantuan to undertake, and discussions have been on again and off again. Nonetheless, environmentalists, sentimentalists, tourists and pilgrims all hope that a plan will be devised and the Dead Sea will be saved.

THE DISCOVERY OF
THE DEAD SEA SCROLLS

In the early spring of 1947, a young Bedouin boy made a startling discovery in one of the more than 250 caves that riddle the hills of this area. In an attempt to retrieve a lost sheep, he wandered into a lonely cave and discovered the seven most famous scrolls in the world, the first of many finds that make up the Dead Sea Scrolls. Unaware of the importance of these manuscripts, the lad took them to a Bethlehem merchant and antique dealer named Kando. Four of the scrolls were purchased from this dealer by the Archbishop Metropolitan Samuel of the Syrian Orthodox Church in Jerusalem. The other three were purchased by the Israeli archaeologist Dr. E. L. Sukenik. Subsequently the Dead Sea Scrolls became known as "the greatest archaeological discovery of the twentieth century."

But why are the scrolls so important? Because they are dated between 200 B.C. and A.D. 100. The manuscripts from which our Old Testament is translated date to about A.D. 1000. Although the Dead Sea Scrolls were written about 1000 years earlier than these were, both are almost identical. This wonderfully validates the accuracy of the Bible. For that reason these scrolls are extremely important. In fact, a special museum at the Hebrew University was built just to house these scrolls. It is known as THE SHRINE OF THE BOOK.

and wash out your bathing suit in fresh water. If you don't, the oily salt on your skin will dry to a hardness that can be scraped off with a knife. But don't let the salt dissuade you. Go for a swim. You'll never experience anything like it. You'll return home and try to describe it to your friends, but you won't be able to.

QUMRAN

Who hasn't heard of the Dead Sea Scrolls? Perhaps no one. But do you know where they were discovered?

As you drive along the northwest shore of the Dead Sea, about ten miles south of Jericho, you'll notice that the sharpness of the sandy-brown mountains changes to a reddish-brown hue and the mountains become a marly plateau. This is where the Dead Sea Scrolls were discovered. When you enter the gate, you'll pass the little guardhouse on your right and drive up the long hill to Qumran.

Adjacent to the hills in which the scrolls were found and just to your left as you ascend the hill from the seashore, you come to the ruins of ancient QUMRAN. Here a monastic community of Jews known as the Essenes once lived. This highly disciplined sect moved from the city life of Jerusalem to the loneliness of the Judaean wilderness in order to lead a more devout and holy life. The Essenes were the ones who painstakingly copied the Dead Sea Scrolls.

The site of Qumram was believed to be one of the "towers in the desert" built by King Uzziah in the eighth or seventh century B.C. (II Chronicles 26:10), and it has been occupied sporadically over the centuries.

The major settlement was initiated during the days of the Maccabees, but the site was abandoned after an earthquake in 31 B.C. If you look at one of the larger square cisterns on the sea side of the site, you will see a huge crack in the stairway leading down to the bottom of the cistern. This is evidence of the great earthquake. Take the best picture of this from the north side of the cistern, with the sea to your left.

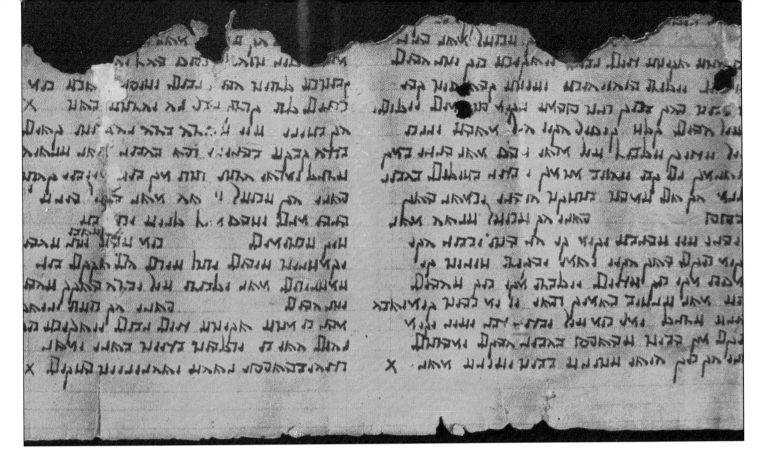

Qumran was again occupied around the time of Herod the Great's death in 4 B.C. The Essenes fled before the advance of Vespasian and the Roman armies in A.D. 68. Its final occupation by the Jewish zealots of Bar Kochba was in A.D. 132-135.

Today the abandoned ruins are like an outdoor, walk-through museum. A guide will escort you through the Qumran village, but anyone with a plan of the city and a knowledge of its history can do just as well. You enter to the right of a tower at the north edge of the ruins. If you climb the tower, you will get a good view of the village layout. The climb isn't difficult, only a dozen steps or so.

One of the most striking features of this community is the outline of the aqueduct system, which brought treasured water from the western hills to be stored in the village's cisterns. You can easily trace it through the city. From your perspective above the partially excavated and restored ruins you can see that the village resembles a maze. As you cut left and right through the ill-defined passageways, you will discover a bakery, a potter's kiln, the community dining hall, a storehouse, workshops, a kitchen, a pantry and numerous cisterns. One of the most interesting rooms is the long and narrow scriptorium. It has stone benches on both sides. It was here that the Dead Sea Scrolls were copied.

The community was built on the edge of a marly cliff. Walk to the very edge of that cliff. Across a deep ravine, which has been cut into the plateau by the restless waters of an adjacent wadi, you can see a cave cut into the side of a neighboring cliff. This is the famous Cave 4 where hundreds of thousands of bits and fragments of scrolls were discovered by archaeologists. Imagine yourself trying to piece together a gigantic puzzle with more than 100,000 pieces. And what's worse, imagine that these pieces were from hundreds of different puzzles, all dumped together in a cave. That's the task that Israeli archaeologists are still undertaking in the reconstruction of the many manuscripts of the Dead Sea Scrolls.

The scrolls were apparently hurriedly hid in this cave when the armies of Rome's Tenth Legion came into view. Over the centuries they have been deteriorating. Unfortunately, you cannot climb down into the cave, for it is steep and slippery and there are no handrails or stairs. Should you slip, the drop to the bottom of the ravine would be deadly. I climbed down into Cave 4 several years ago and found that all the parchment and pottery fragments had been removed.

As you make your way back to the parking lot and the large sunshelters, look off to the distant hills north of Qumran. There, with a little help from the guide or the soda salesman, you can spot Cave 1, where the Bedouin shepherd first discovered the Dead Sea Scrolls.

EIN FASHKHA/EIN GEDI

About three miles south of Qumran is a pleasant oasis called EIN FASHKHA. This island of coolness in a sea of sun will quickly refresh you from your visit to the shadeless city of the Essenes. There is a clinic nearby specifically for those who become ill from overexposure to the sun. A few minutes in Ein Fashkha will be all the medicine you need.

This beautiful spot is a favorite of the Israelis today. On the weekends it's so crowded that it's almost impossible to move. Ein Fashkha features a circular pool about 30 feet in diameter, filled with fresh water flowing

Below: The springs of Ein Fashkha

Opposite: Ein Gedi Falls at Ein Gedi

from the mountains. There are also three pools just for the children. Not only do these pools provide restoration from the hot sun but the modern dressing rooms and rest rooms provide a place to shower and change after a dip in the nearby Dead Sea. Centuries ago the Qumran Essenes used this oasis area to grow food for their ascetic brotherhood. Can you imagine the chagrin on the faces of these pietists if they could see their nature preserve used by the fun-frolickers of the Dead Sea?

Ten miles south of Ein Fashkha, approximately halfway down on the western shore of the Dead Sea, there is another oasis—EIN GEDI, also spelled "En Gedi." Here a half-hour climb brings you to some very delightful waterfalls, with fresh-water pools and an incredible view of the Dead Sea.

A new kibbutz, also called Ein Gedi, lies between the spring of Ein Gedi and the Dead Sea. Here vegetables, date palms and other vegetation grow in profusion adjacent to the wastelands of sand and the wastewaters of the Dead Sea. How is this possible? The answer is DAVID'S FOUNTAIN.

In the days of the Old Testament, this area in the territory of Judah (Joshua 15:62) was known as Hazazontamar (II Chronicles 20:2). Here the mountains meet the sea, and the cliffs rise above the sand nearly 2000 feet. These sharp, flat-faced cliffs are peppered

EIN GEDI AND QUMRAN

There is a similarity between modern Ein Gedi and ancient Qumran that is ironic. In the Ein Gedi Kibbutz there is a community that has abandoned city ways to live in a brotherhood by the sea. This was true of Qumran. In the Ein Gedi Kibbutz there is a spirit of defiance—defiance of the arid land, of the nearby adversaries and of the acceptable lifestyle. This was true of Qumran. History has a strange way of repeating itself. In fact, many modern Israelis consider the Essene community at Qumran to be "the world's oldest Kibbutz."

with caves and dens. David and his men took refuge from King Saul in one of these caves, and it was here that David spared Saul's life after he cut off a piece of his garment while Saul slept (I Samuel 24).

This area is fertile because of the springs and a stream that bring water in abundance from the limestone cliffs to the west. The stream has come to be known as David's Fountain because of the importance of this area in the early life of David. The fruitful vineyards and luxuriant growth of the area are praised in The Song of Solomon 1:14.

To get to the waterfalls you must go to the parking lot and follow the signs of the nature trail. On the way you will see rock formations of the desert hills that are absolutely otherworldly. After about 30 minutes of steady climbing, you will arrive at the fabulous Ein Gedi waterfalls. Here, in a canyon of green vegetation, the water tumbles from a height of 300 feet and leaves you breathless. Stand under the falls and let the water cascade over you like a heavenly shower. There is no feeling in the world more invigorating, especially on a hot day.

MASADA

As you drive south along the Dead Sea, you come next to MASADA. This National Parks Authority site is one of the most significant landmarks in all Israel. Masada is to the Israeli what the Alamo or Pearl Harbor is to the American. Masada is a symbol of dynamic leadership and a stalwart defense in the face of insurmountable odds and certain death. Here the oath of allegiance is taken by all the cadet graduates of Israel's military academy—"Masada shall not fall again." This is not just a cadet slogan; it is Israel's national determination.

Masada is an immense flat-topped plateau that from a distance resembles a gigantic thumb pushing its way up through the earth's crust. It is an enormous aneurysm on the geological depression called the Jordan Valley. Located some two and one-half miles from the western shore of the Dead Sea, exactly opposite "The Tongue," Masada is a half mile long and 220 yards wide. It is a rock fortress, the top of which rises to about sea level, while the valley, 1320 feet below it, remains the lowest spot on earth.

It is possible that Masada (also spelled Massada) is mentioned in the Bible. First Samuel 24:22 records that when David fled from the threats of the jealous King Saul, "David and his men went up to the stronghold" (I Chronicles 12:8). The word translated "stronghold" is the Hebrew word Metsade, the equivalent of Masada. However, this sandy-brown crag did not really become important until the days of Herod the Great. Herod, who reigned 37—4 B.C., was the prolific builder of Caesarea, Samaria and Jericho. He also established a winter palace at Masada. This combination fortress/palace was considered to be Herod's strongest. Around the perimeter of the plateau's top, he erected an 18-foot-high wall with 38 towers, each 75 feet high. Not only was the site nearly inaccessible; it was also nearly impregnable.

Today there are three ways to ascend to the top of this rectangular rock. Usually only two of these are used by tourists. The third, the ramp path known as "The Battery," is on the west side of Masada and is approachable only by a road from Arad.

The first method is to climb Masada from the east—if you are a hardy soul. Here you will find a two-mile-long serpentine path, the Snake Path. It is steep, filled with hairpin curves; and it places an unusual strain on body muscles. You need to allow about two hours for the climb.

The second method, the cable car, affords a breathtaking ride and deposits you just 75 short steps from the summit.

To support his summer palace, Herod the Great developed an ingenious system of aqueducts and cisterns to catch and retain every

Above: **Cable car to the top of Masada**

Below: **Herod's palace at Masada**

precious drop of water that fell on this arid area. Around the perimeter of Masada's heights you can see a series of pools, baths and cisterns. One of the cisterns is estimated to have held 80,000 gallons of water.

At the top of Masada, you will see the royal family's residence, the officers' quarters, an administration building, the Zealot quarters and a Byzantine church, as well as a synagogue, the world's oldest. You can buy a plan of the site very inexpensively at the shop on the ground level or at the entranceway on the top.

There are two things you dare not miss at Masada. The first is the Roman bath adjacent to the partially restored storehouses at the northern end of the rock. The second is the northern palace.

The luxurious bathhouse was built by Herod the Great according to the customary Roman pattern. You enter through the large courtyard that faces the northern palace. Originally this area was surrounded by pillars on three sides. The floor was a red-white-and-black mosaic. The first room you enter is the dressing room (apoditerium), which has frescoes

View from Herod's palace at Masada

on the walls. Through a doorway you see a three-chambered bathhouse, the most interesting room at Masada. To your right is the cold-water bath (frigidarium); ahead is the warm-water bath (tepidarium); and to your left, the steam room for hot-water baths (caldarium).

As you stand on the walkway overlooking the floor, you need to reconstruct the room in your mind. On the floor are more than 200 tiny pillars made of round clay bricks, each pillar approximately two feet high and six to eight inches in diameter. These pillars originally supported a suspended mosaic floor. Adjacent to the caldarium was an oven. From this oven hot air would flow through pipes into the space beneath the suspended floor. Since the room was nearly airtight, the floor would warm quickly, heating the entire room. When water was poured on the heated floor, it turned the hot room into a steam bath. Herod had all the comforts of home at his winter residence.

The Northern Palace of King Herod was built on three levels. Level two was 40 feet below the first level, while level three was 70 feet below the first level. The three terraces housed Herod's private villa. (The Western Palace was the official residence.)

You enter the upper terrace from the side near the Dead Sea. Here was Herod's living room. The walls were highly decorated with colorful frescoes of which, unfortunately, almost nothing remains. The floor was covered with a black-and-white mosaic. Because this entire residential area is so small, it is assumed that it was intended for Herod alone, or perhaps for himself and one of his nine wives.

Walk to the very northern edge of the upper terrace. Here you will find a rounded balcony, the pride of the palace. Imagine you are the Idumaean king himself. From this semicircular porch you would get an absolutely breathtaking view to the north, east and west. You could see Ein Gedi and beyond. In fact, on a clear day you could see all the way to Jericho and to your palace there.

MASADA: HEROISM AND TRAGEDY

Every school child in Israel has made the climb to the stronghold's summit to hear the story of the drama of Masada. The events are both heroic and tragic.

Herod's magnificent palace eventually became occupied by a small Roman garrison. During the Jewish revolt of A.D. 66, a band of zealots surprised the soldiers in a sneak attack and overpowered them. From this elevated sanctuary they waged a guerrilla war against the Romans. They had no fear of reprisal, for Masada was easily defended, and the surface of the plateau yielded enough grain and vegetables to keep the vast storerooms well stocked. This army of Jewish freedom fighters could continue to harass the Roman invaders as long as they wished.

But the power and pride of Rome was not to be denied. The emperor knew that, even though Jerusalem had been destroyed in A.D. 70, as long as these outlaw Jews continued to occupy Masada, a spark of hope beat in every Hebrew heart. The zealots of Masada had become folk heroes, and they must be defeated.

This seemingly impossible task fell to the Roman general Flavius Silva. Despite a three-year siege, from A.D. 70—73, Silva was unsuccessful at driving the zealots from the fortress. The Romans used every device they had—rock bombardments, battering rams, flaming torches, siege machines and more. Nothing worked. Then they undertook the long and arduous task of building an earthen ramp from the floor of the valley to the western crest of Masada. The ramp is attached to Masada just below the western palace. If you stand at the western wall or the northern palace outlook, you will easily discern the remains of the ramp. It was truly an amazing feat, considering the tons and tons of earth the Romans had to move in order to build such a ramp.

With the ramp completed and the Romans literally at their door, it was only a matter of time for the zealots. Their leader, Eliezer Ben Yair, delivered an impassioned appeal to his fortress followers, saying that it would be far more honorable for Masada's doomed defenders to die by their own hands than be tortured and sold into slavery by the Romans. All agreed. When the final Roman assault came the next morning, it was met with no resistance, only a deafening silence. Suddenly the horrible truth was evident. One of history's largest mass suicides had taken place during the night. The bodies of 960 men, women and children were lying side by side, in family groups. They were the victims of being too small in number and too large in pride. "Masada shall not fall again."

Roman ramp leading to the top of Masada

The descent to the middle and lower terrace levels is on the southwest side and is not always open to the public. On the middle level you see a circular structure that originally consisted of two concentric walls. These walls served as bases for some sort of a columned structure. Apparently this was Herod's leisure or relaxation center—his family room. On the west side of this bunga-low-sized level is a perfectly preserved staircase leading to the upper terrace.

The lower terrace consists of a rectangular area about the same size as the middle terrace. Its remains are the best preserved. On the facade of the lime rock of the southern wall, columns with Corinthian capitals are plastered. The walls are painted with three-foot-high red-and-green frescoes that are designed to give the appearance of paneled marble facing. On the east side, steps lead down to a small but elaborate private bath with a frigidarium, tepidarium and a caldarium. When the site was excavated, the skeletons of a man, woman and child were discovered here. The archaeologists involved were surely reminded of the chilling story of the last tragic night of Masada.

Before you leave the top of this remarkable rock, take one final panoramic view of the lower Jordan Valley. From the western edge you can see the southernmost ridges of the Central Highlands, the hills of Judaea and Idumaea. These dark and forboding mountains soon level to the uplands of the Negev, visible from the southern tip of Masada. Standing at the eastern lookout, you get a perfect view of the Dead Sea, the Lisan Peninsula, "The Tongue" and the mountains of Moab. Notice how placid the sea appears, how shallow the southern extremity is and how the Valley of Salt flattens out from the lower tip of the sea. From your vantage point you can see the mountains to your east and west. You begin to appreciate just how deep the Jordan Valley and the Dead Sea really are. To the north you can see the valley stretch along the sea and wonder what the Jewish zealots must have felt as they saw the Roman armies ap-

Possibly the area of ancient Sodom

proaching their stronghold.

Perhaps as you leave this hallowed site you will be treated to one more demonstration of determination. Frequently the mighty Israeli air force flies these skies on training missions. Whenever I have seen Israeli jets streak above the heights of Masada, they have tipped their wings in tribute to their respect for Masada.

SODOM

Just south of Masada the road along the western shore of the Dead Sea forks to the right. This highway winds west to ARAD and finally joins the main road of the Negev that links Beersheba with Jerusalem.

If you continue on the Dead Sea road to the south, you will pass an oasis named "EIN BOKEK." Here you will find a guest house and a health resort. Its baths are fed by the hot springs of HAMEI-ZOHAR to the south. Above the resort you can spot the ruins of the Bokek Fort, built to defend the freshwater spring. Two miles south, at Hamei-Zohar, there are additional bath houses and a clinic. The hot mineral springs of this area, frequented by David and Solomon, today provide comfort for all sorts of ailments. Doctors at the clinic claim particular success in curing diseases of the joints, allergies and disorders of the skin. Just south of Zohar the road branches back to the right toward Arad. If you contin-

ue south along the sea, however, you will soon be near the site of Sodom.

It is important to remember that a visit to SODOM is not a visit to a city or even to some ruins. The wicked city of Sodom is no more. Once five cities dotted this plain: Sodom, Gomorrah, Admah, Bela (Zoar) and Zeboiim (Genesis 14:2-11). It was in this region of the Plain of Jordan that Lot "pitched his tent even as far as Sodom" (Genesis 13:12). But the Bible pointedly says that "the men of Sodom were exceedingly wicked and sinful against the LORD" (Genesis 13:13). The sins the men of Sodom committed have always been despicable and condemned by God. Thus the Almighty destroyed the cities of the plain by raining brimstone and fire down from heaven so that "the smoke of the land went up like the smoke of a furnace" (Genesis 19:24-29). Since that day Sodom has been used as a symbol of judgment by God. Moses (Deuteronomy 29:23), Isaiah (13:19), Jeremiah (50:40), Amos (4:11), Zephaniah (2:9), Jude (1:4-7) and even Jesus Christ (Matthew 10:15) used its destruction as a warning.

Today archaeologists believe that the remains of the ruined city lie somewhere beneath the shallow end of the Dead Sea. Hence the drive to Sodom doesn't produce the same kind of results that the drive to other biblical sites does. What you do see as you approach the area are some of the world's most desolate deserts, tortured mountains, salt-encrusted seashores and bizarre shapes. Rising from the shallow waters of the Dead Sea are rocks and driftwood, sealed with centuries of saline solutions. Many of them look like agonizing albino octopuses, gasping for breath as they struggle to be loosed from the bottom of the sea.

The noxious smell of sulphur fills the air above the Dead Sea Works' potash and bromide plants, which now make up the only semblance of civilized life at Sodom. This is part of Israel's $545 million program to mine the country's most valuable natural resource—the Dead Sea. In addition to its high (33-50) percentage of salt, the Dead Sea also contains billions of tons of potassium chloride, magnesium bromide, sodium chloride, magnesium chloride, calcium chloride and sulphur. In fact, the Dead Sea is so rich in mineral content that it has enough potassium chloride to supply the world's need for potash fertilizer for 3000 years. This is not only the lowest spot on earth. It is also the richest. Nasty and noxious as it is, the Dead Sea is worth incalculable billions of dollars. All of these minerals are slated for extraction from the sea, by both the Israeli and Jordanian governments.

A couple of miles to the north, along the main road, you will see numerous salt mines and the famous CAVE OF SODOM. Now closed for safety reasons, the cave is a labyrinth of salt-studded passageways and acrid stalactites. Above the cave is a natural outcropping of stone that has been pointed out to travelers as the stony remains of Lot's curious wife (Genesis 19:26). Even if you have a vivid imagination, you cannot see that the stone pillar resembles a feminine figure.

Along this road also is a post office. Travelers go out of their way to have their letters postmarked here. The post office stamp says, "Lowest Point on Earth." This is an apt description for the southern end of the Great Rift and the unique Jordan Valley.

CHAPTER NINE

THE WILD, WILD SOUTH

CITIES OF THE NEGEV

"And afterward the children of Judah went down to fight against the Canaanites who dwelt in the mountains, in the South, and in the lowland. Then Judah went against the Canaanites who dwelt in Hebron."

Judges 1:9,10

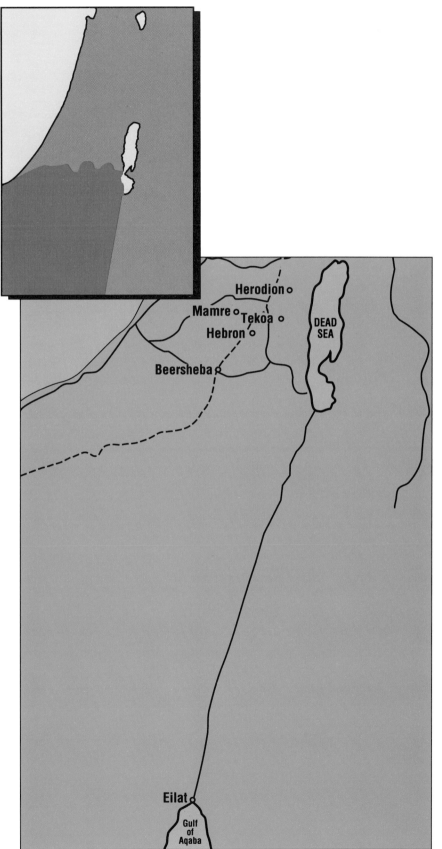

According to the Talmudic scholars, the word "Negev" means "dry." Old Testament scholars disagree. The Bible refers to the Negev as the "south" (Genesis 12:9). Both are true. The Negev is the dry south (Deuteronomy 1:7; 34:3; Joshua 15:19; Judges 1:15). But if you're expecting to see unending dunes of monotonous sand, you'll be disappointed.

The Negev is wild and raging, a varying landscape of saw-toothed mountains, wind-sculptured valleys, eroded gorges and a formidable wilderness. Here you will see huge boulders of black volcanic rock and craggy mounds of sandstone that look like the jaws of a shark piercing the surface of the ocean. The whole region is a rainbow of yellows, browns, reds and blacks.

Some years ago the Negev encroached upon the cities of the south. But today adventurous Israeli settlers have pummeled the Negev into submission and rolled back the encroaching sands like the lid on a tin of sardines. Beyond the modern settlements, however, the Negev is still the wild, wild south. These wilderness crags are the home of the Bedouins who roam the Negev, much like Abraham did millennia ago (Genesis 12:9;

Above: **Herodion**

Right: **View from Herodion**

13:1). With temperatures ranging from 125 degrees during the day to 50 degrees during cold winter nights, the region is as inhospitable today as it was when Hagar fled the jealousy of Sarah (Genesis 16:7-16).

HERODION

As you leave Jerusalem and head south for Bethlehem, a secondary road just north of the City of David takes you east and then south through barren hills to HERODION. You can't miss Herodion; it's the cone-shaped mountain that looks just like a volcano. It's clearly visible from Jerusalem, Bethlehem and just about everywhere else in this part of the Judean mountains.

Actually, Herodion (also spelled Herodium) is a man-made mountain, a product of that prolific builder—Herod the Great. In a colossal earthmoving project, Herod piled up tons of dirt to form it. At its foot he then built palaces, pools and beautifully terraced gardens. It became a retreat and fortress, like his other massive building projects, such as Masada and Hyrcanus. A product of typical Herodian extravagance, it must have been a sight to behold.

As you approach Herodion, you must park in the elevated parking lot at the base of the manufactured mountain. A path winds clockwise up the side of the mound. Beyond the entrance house is a series of some 200 white marble steps that lead to the citadel. Once you enter the citadel, you will see four gigantic towers at the corners—three semicircular and one round. The courtyard between these towers is surrounded by Corinthian columns, now of varying heights. There are numerous baths and reservoirs, as in Herod's other palaces, and the Herodion dining room even has a synagogue.

The outer diameter of this cone is 180 feet. If you climb to its cap, you can walk around the perimeter of the mound. This enables you to see the courtyard in detail. Even better, the view from here is absolutely incredible. Look toward the east and you will see a gap between the nearby wilderness of Judaea and the faraway mountains of Moab. This is the Jordan Valley. While you cannot see the valley because it is too low, you can definitely detect that it's out there. To the south is wilderness and desert. To the north and west are rolling hills, with Jerusalem off in the distance. The climb to the top of the Herodian is well worth it, if only for the spectacular view.

Although Herod died at his palace in Jericho, his body was brought to Herodian 15 days later for burial. King Herod, himself a

half-Jew, tried to kill the King of the Jews by ordering the slaughter of innocent children (Matthew 2:16). Isn't it ironic that he is buried just four miles southeast of Bethlehem, the city of Jesus' birth? While few travelers come to the city of Herod's burial, millions journey each year to the city of Christ's birth.

TEKOA

As you continue on the secondary road south from Herodion, you quickly come to the site of ancient TEKOA. Not much is to be seen here today except some simple ruins that cover about five acres. Located approximately equidistant between Jerusalem and Hebron, Tekoa is 2800 feet above sea level. It is situated on the edge of the rugged and desolate wilderness to the east. Here the terrain is barely passable. You can almost picture the Prophet Amos tending his sheep in these mountainous crags before he was called by God (Amos 1:1; 7:14).

Joab sent for a woman from Tekoa to feign being a mourner in order to get David to reconcile with his estranged son Absalom (II Samuel 14). Later, Rehoboam fortified this town (II Chronicles 11:6). When King Jehoshaphat was confronted with a multitude of Moabites and Ammonites, the prophet Jahaziel assured Jehoshaphat that "the battle is not yours, but God's" (II Chronicles 20:14-16). The armies of Israel "rose early in the morning and went out into the wilderness of Tekoa, singing and praising the Lord in the face of the enemy" (vv. 21,22). The wilderness

of Tekoa hasn't changed much since Jehoshaphat's day.

The road winds through the village of SEIR, where tradition says Esau is buried. In about three minutes you pass through HALHUL or "Halhool." This Canaanite town, which became the possession of Judah (Joshua 15:1,58), is the highest village in the country. Along the road you will see some roadside vegetable and fruit stands. Traffic then gets heavier, for you are coming closer to the main highway.

The secondary road joins the main road from Jerusalem just north of Hebron. There you arrive in the famous VALLEY OF ESHCOL. "Eshcol" means "cluster of grapes."

This is the valley from which the men who were sent by Moses to spy out the Promised Land carried back a cluster of grapes (Numbers 13:23,24). Today, all around the Holy Land, you can see poles with the black silhouette of two pointy-bearded men bearing an enormous cluster of grapes. This has become the official tourist emblem of Israel, and it is worn as a medallion by every official guide in Israel. Grapes are still grown in

Above: Herds of Tekoa

Below: The Valley of Eshcol

abundance here today. The topographical change from the wilderness of Tekoa to the Valley of Eshcol is quite abrupt.

MAMRE

Just before you arrive at Hebron, there is a tiny road that forks back to the left toward the eastern wilderness. The highway sign guides you to "Ramat Al Khaled," which is Arabic for "the high place of the friend"—a reference to Abraham. Here you will see an enclosure marking the traditional site of the OAK OF MAMRE, or Abraham's Oak.

The Book of Genesis records that when Abraham returned from his sojourn in Egypt he "moved his tent, and went and dwelt by the terebinth trees of Mamre, which are in Hebron, and built an altar there to the LORD" (Genesis 13:18). Later, after his separation from Lot, Abraham was in Mamre resting under an oak tree when three angels approached him and apprised him of the imminent destruction of Sodom and Gomorrah (Genesis 18).

The site is protected by a vast 150-by-200-foot enclosure that includes walls constructed by Herod the Great. Destroyed by Vespasian in A.D. 68, this enclosure was rebuilt by the Roman Emperor Hadrian in the second century A.D. and made a pagan cult center. Constantine removed Hadrian's altar and built a basilica on the site. You can still see traces of the ruins of this church. In the southwest corner is the WELL OF ABRAHAM, a place where shepherds for centuries have watered their sheep. But of greatest interest by far is a huge, twisted, ancient oak tree. It is unlikely that this oak is the one under which Abraham rested, for it doesn't appear to be old enough. It does commemorate well the site and provides a worthy photo by which to remember Mamre.

After you get back on the main road, the highway splits. The right fork is the express

Abraham's Well at Beersheba

road to Beersheba. The left road enters Hebron. Go left and take a step back in time.

HEBRON

As you enter Hebron, you pass some beautiful villas and a few local shops. The real shopping at Hebron, however, is ahead. Hebron is known for its manufacturing of glass. Up ahead on the left is a glass-blowing factory, next to a pottery factory and a woodworking factory. Here is Hebron's haven for happy shoppers. The little glass-blown items are especially interesting.

The Hebron market is the center of activity, not only for Hebron but for the entire Negev hinterland. Here you will see black-clad Bedouins sitting around, smoking water pipes, swapping tales and bartering for goods. The marketing of goatskins for water carriers and sheepskin vests and jackets is big business. The market has all the sights, sounds and especially the smells of a sheepherders' market.

Abraham's tomb is located in Hebron. Go past Hebron's shopping areas and follow the streets to the left. There you will find the final earthly resting place of the man who "waited for the city which has foundations, whose builder and maker is God" (Hebrews 11:10).

Genesis 23 relates that "Sarah died in Kirjath Arba (that is, Hebron) in the land of Canaan . . . and Abraham . . . spoke to the sons of Heth, saying . . . 'Give me a property for a burial place . . . give me the cave of Machpelah.' . . . And after this, Abraham buried Sarah his wife in the cave of the field of Machpelah before Mamre (that is, Hebron) in the land of Canaan" (23:2-4,9,19).

The CAVE OF MACHPELAH brings to Hebron the designation and distinction of being one of Israel's four "Holy Cities." (The others are Jerusalem, Tiberias and Safed.) The cave today is a fortress-like mosque of huge proportions. Built originally by Herod the Great and later added to by the Mamelukes, the windowless hulk measures 193 feet by 112 feet. The walls of this mosque are 40 to 60 feet high.

The Cave of Machpelah is itself inaccessible. But if you climb the steps leading to the mosque and enter the steel-grey building, you will see a series of cenotaphs. (A cenotaph is a commemorative monument erected in honor of a person buried elsewhere.) These are said to be located over the actual graves of the patriarchs. Though no one may enter the cave, we can get a brief glimpse of it under a pillared dome near the cenotaphs of Isaac and Rebekah.

The inside of the mosque is beautifully decorated with inlaid wood and intricate mosaic walls. The cenotaphs of Isaac and Rebekah are located in the main section of the mosque, the large room to the south. In an adjoining open courtyard, behind a silver grating, you can see the cenotaphs of Abraham and Sarah. They are covered with gold-embroidered velvet. Opposite, in the northernmost room, are the cenotaphs of Jacob and Leah. This room features a 700-year-old stained-glass window. Next door to the west is a cenotaph for Joseph, although most agree that the body of Joseph is buried at Nablus.

The city of Hebron is the southernmost city of the hill country of Judaea and the Central Highlands. From here the land drops off rapidly to the east but only gradually to

The Cave of Machpelah in Hebron

HEBRON IN HISTORY

The Old Testament contains numerous references to HEBRON. In Hebron Ishmael was born (Genesis 16). All three of the patriarchs lived here (Genesis 35:27; 37:1). Joseph left Hebron in search of his brothers, whom he eventually found in Dothan (Genesis 37:14-17). Jacob and his sons journeyed from here to Beersheba and then to Egypt (Genesis 46). Four centuries later Moses sent spies to Hebron to survey the land (Numbers 13:17-25). Hebron and its king were captured by Joshua (Joshua 10), and the city was given as an inheritance to Caleb (Joshua 15:13). It was both a Levitical city of Judah (Joshua 15:54) and a city of refuge (Joshua 20:7).

David was anointed king over Judah, and then all Israel, not at Jerusalem but at Hebron. Hebron became David's first capital city (II Samuel 2:1-4,10,11; 5:1-5; I Kings 2:11). Abner was treacherously killed by Joab at its gates. This prepared the way for David's ascendancy to the throne (II Samuel 3:27-29). David slew Ishbosheth's murderers here (II Samuel 4:5-12). Absalom organized his revolt against his father, David, in Hebron (II Samuel 15:7-12).

Hebron has been a violent city for nearly all of its existence. During the first Jewish revolt the Roman general Titus destroyed Hebron, as well as Jerusalem. In the years since, the city has been under the domination of one faction after another. In 1929, a bloody slaughter occurred which decimated the Jewish population. Since that time the city has been almost exclusively Arab. Today the Israelis call the Hebronites citizens of the West Bank; the Jordanians claim that they belong to the Hashemite Kingdom of Jordan. But if you ask a Bedouin of Hebron who he is, he will say he is a Palestinian. In the maelstrom of politics, religion and war, the simple people of Hebron are struggling with exactly where they fit in the mysterious puzzle we call the Middle East.

BEERSHEBA

Some 28 miles southwest of Hebron is BEERSHEBA (also spelled "Beer-Sheva"). During the days of the patriarchs this was only a cluster of wells. It is the last watering hole before the desert of the Negev. Here the luster of the green hills turns to the brown of the windswept sands. While Hebron is 3042 feet above sea level, the elevation of Beersheba is only 950 feet.

Beersheba, once a wild and unruly city nicknamed "Dodge City," is the gateway to the Negev. Today the town is being tamed by growing housing developments, subdivisions and municipal buildings. "Dodge City" has become the capital of the Negev.

When the Israelis captured the city of Beersheba from the Egyptians in 1948, it was a village of 3000 people. But the stouthearted

the west and south. The road to Beersheba slopes through patches of rich soil and fertile grazing land. It is a beautiful drive.

Right: **Tell Beersheba**

Zionists saw settling this city as a particular challenge in taming the wilderness and rolling back the desert. Today the city has a population of 113,000. It presents a striking contrast between the hustle and bustle of the big city and the slow moving, water-pipe-smoking nomadic life of the nearby Bedouins. It is a microcosm of Israel, some of the old, some of the new.

A visit to Tell Beersheba, two or three miles northeast of the modern city, is worth your while. The excavation was begun in 1969 and realistically portrays the life and work of twentieth-century archaeologists.

But the major reason to travel to Beersheba is the BEDOUIN MARKET. Don't come to Beersheba unless it's Thursday. It's the only day the market is open, the day Bedouin tribes come from the Negev to buy, sell and trade at the flavorful marketplace.

If you walk through the center of town and take a left turn at the far edge of the old city, your nose will take you the rest of the way. What do the Bedouins sell or trade? You name it—camels, sheep, donkeys, skins, vegetables, jewelry, flour, coffee, tobacco, handwoven rugs. You may even be able to join the fracas and do some haggling. But you must get there

BEERSHEBA IN THE BIBLE

The name Beersheba means "the well of seven," or "the well of the oath." It was here that Abraham and Abimelech, king of Gerar, pledged mutual allegiance: "Therefore he called that place Beersheba; because the two of them swore an oath there" (Genesis 21:31).

Traditionally, Beersheba has been not only the southern border of Judah's territory (Joshua 25:28; Judges 10:1; I Samuel 3:20) but the southern border of the Promised Land itself, as the expression "from Dan to Beersheba" indicates.

Like Hebron, Beersheba is biblically important. It was the home of Abraham for a time (Genesis 22:19). Both he and his son Isaac made a covenant with Abimelech here (Genesis 21:22-34; Genesis 26:23-33). Here God appeared to both Isaac (Genesis 26:23-25) and Jacob (Genesis 46:1-7). Jacob fled from Beersheba to Haran to escape the anger of his brother Esau (Genesis 28:10). And on his journey to live with his son Joseph in Egypt, Jacob delayed in Beersheba long enough to offer sacrifices to Jehovah (Genesis 46:1-5). Finally, when the Prophet Elijah fled from Mount Carmel to escape the wicked queen Jezebel, it was here, in Beersheba, that he sat down under a juniper tree and sulked. Here, too, the angel of the Lord fed him in preparation for his journey of 40 days and nights to Mount Horeb (I Kings 19:1-8).

early. The market opens about 5 o'clock a.m. and closes before noon. It's an experience you won't forget.

You have now traversed Bible Country "from Dan to Beersheba." There is one more city in the extreme south you shouldn't miss.

EILAT

If you drive on the road south out of Beersheba toward Eilat, you must be ready to experience the desert. The 140-mile drive is pleasant if you have air conditioning, but without it the temperatures—which can reach 125 degrees Fahrenheit during the day—can

Well of the Oath, at Beersheba

Above: Road to Timna Valley

Right: Solomon's Pillars, on the edge of the Timna Valley, are formations of redstone more than 150 feet high.

modern Eilat. Wisely, Solomon used the north winds that howled down through the Arabah (Rift Valley) to fire his smelting furnaces.

In Bible times, EILAT (locally known as ELAT) was two separate towns—Ezion-geber and Elath, or Eloth. Ezion-geber was the terminal port of Solomon's trading ventures through the Red Sea. First Kings 9:26 says, "King Solomon also built a fleet of ships in Ezion-Geber, which is near Elath on the shore of the Red sea, in the land of Edom." From here the Israelite king traded for spices and gold with Ophir and Arabia. Perhaps this is where the Queen of Sheba docked when she paid her famous visit.

Today Eilat is known for another kind of gold—sunshine. The sun shines almost 365

be cruel. Regular air service exists between Jerusalem and Eilat. You may wish to explore this alternative. I have made the trip both ways and enjoyed them equally.

About 18 miles north of Eilat is the TIMNA VALLEY. SOLOMON'S PILLARS are just a few minutes west of the main road to Eilat. These pillars of Nubian sandstone are half as high as a football field is long, and they resemble stone sentinels watching over the valley. They are tinted with subtle shades of pink, yellow, cream and white. Carved by wind erosion, they are a testimony to the power of the wind in this region. Around the corner to your right is the outline of a former Egyptian-Kenite temple that dates from the thirteenth century B.C., near the time of the Jews' exodus from Egypt.

On the main road and not much farther south is the entrance to the TIMNA COPPER MINES. These were opened in 1955 and reopened in 1980.

Just west of these modern mines are mines of the Early Bronze Age, the KING SOLOMON'S MINES. These are the earliest shaft and gallery mines discovered to date in the Holy Land, and they appear to have been Egyptian in origin. However, it is well known that King Solomon mined this area and operated both a copper-smelting and iron-smelting refinery at Ezion-geber, a site just west of

days a year here, and Eilat has become a favorite spot for Europeans who want to get away from the cold winters. The people of Eilat are survivors by nature. They are less than a mile from the border with Jordan and the Jordanian seaport city of Aqaba. They are but a few miles from Egypt and the Sinai. If you stand facing the Red Sea and look at a tall smoke stack off in the distance (about 11 o'clock), you are looking at Saudi Arabia. But tucked away neatly between the rugged mountains of Jordan and the sands of the Sinai is the jewel of the Red Sea—Eilat.

There are two kinds of jewels in Eilat. One is the locally mined Eilat stone. This gorgeous green-blue stone is a type of malachite. Local artisans set the stone into items such as earrings, cuff links, rings, necklaces. These are not overly expensive.

The other jewel is comprised of the magnificent emerald-green and aquamarine waters of the Gulf of Elat (Gulf of Aqabah). It contains some of the most wonderful coral in the world. From CORAL BEACH, about two and one-half miles west of the city, to LAGOON BEACH at its eastern edge, you are in for a swimming, snorkeling and sight-seeing treat.

At Coral Beach, multi-colored fish swim in an underwater nature reserve. A glass-bottomed boat tour is available here. If you want to see the bottom of the sea in a less exotic way, try the UNDERWATER OBSERVATORY AND AQUARIUM. The one-story buildings with distinctively rounded roofs enable you to descend beneath the surface of the water and see the exotic tropical fish darting in and out of the coral. Look especially for the rays; they are extremely graceful. This underwater observatory opens up a whole new world. The museum is devoted to fluorescent corals and luminescent fish and is absolutely fascinating.

If your journey to Bible Country calls for a place to stop and relax a while, surely Eilat is the place. As you bask in the sunshine and as you enjoy the cool breezes from the Red Sea and the crystal-clear waters, you may forget that you are only a few miles from neighbors who haven't been on speaking terms with Israel in quite a while. Enjoy it while you can.

CHAPTER TEN

THE HILLS OF ENCHANTMENT

THE ENVIRONS OF JERUSALEM

*"Should you not have obeyed the words which the LORD proclaimed through
the former prophets when Jerusalem and the cities around it were inhabited
and prosperous, and the South and the Lowland were inhabited?"*

Zechariah 7:7

Although it has been said that all roads lead to Rome, in the course of human history it would be more appropriate to say that all roads lead to Jerusalem. In fact, many roads do lead to Jerusalem, literally. In the final analysis, all of them are "up."

The road from the north rides the mountains of the Central Highlands through Nablus and Ramallah and arrives in Jerusalem at the Damascus Gate. The Jericho Road is the famous road leading from the Jordan Valley and climbing to the heights of Jerusalem, arriving at the Kidron Valley. The Bethlehem road leads north across the Hinnom Valley from Bethlehem, Hebron and Beersheba to Jerusalem. The road east from Tel Aviv runs through the Ajalon Valley where Joshua commanded the sun to stand still (Joshua 10:12). This road is still quite new. It was opened July 11, 1979, and is a swift, four-lane highway, which passes the Ben-Gurion Airport.

The environs of Jerusalem hold many enchantments. Just being in the vicinity of Old Jerusalem brings a special excitement. You travel up the hills and down the hills, up and down, finishing the day with dust on your shoes, aches in your legs and joy in your heart.

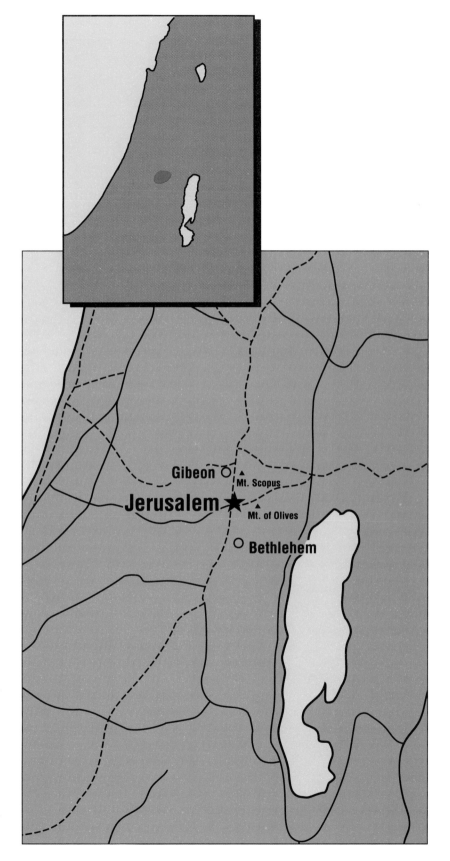

Above: Sanhedrin tombs

Below: Jerusalem from Nabi Samwil

you pass Saint Stephen's Basilica. Bear left to the Central Command Square. This is where the Mandelbaum Gate (Jerusalem's Checkpoint Charlie) stood during the partition days of divided Jerusalem. Then cross the square and continue north on Shmuel Hanavi (Prophet Samuel) Street to the northern Jerusalem suburbs. At Hasanhedrin Street you enter a wooded enclosure containing the SANHEDRIN TOMBS.

Also known as the "Tombs of the Judges," these tombs were discovered in the seventeenth century. They received their name because the main cave contained 66 tombs of members of the Jewish Sanhedrin, Israel's first-century Supreme Court. (Another 22 of the first-century tombs were discovered later.)

The entrance to the rock-hewn tombs exhibits the best preserved rock carving in Jerusalem. As you enter, you can distinguish carvings of pomegranates, citrons and acanthus leaves. Just in front of the entrance there is a basin hollowed out in the cave floor. It was undoubtedly used as a ritual basin for the purification of the dead. Inside there are burial chambers on three levels. The chambers are in burial alcoves, carved in the walls of the rooms off the main passageway. As you make your way outside, you'll leave the tombs through a vestibule, which has stone benches for the mourners.

There are many tombs in the area north of

So that you don't miss any important thing, approach the vicinity of Jerusalem systematically. Start with the environs north of the Old City; then continue your tour east, south and west. Think of the walled city as the center of a clock. Begin at 12 o'clock and work your way clockwise around the area within five or six miles of Old Jerusalem.

THE ENVIRONS NORTH

Leave Jerusalem at the Damascus Gate and travel the Nablus Road north until just after

Mizpeh is actually about three miles farther north, at Tell en-Nasbeh.

If you take the Nablus Road past the ATAROT JERUSALEM AIRPORT, you will come to ancient GIBEON on the right side of the road, less than a mile northwest of Nabi Samwil and only five miles north of Jerusalem.

At Gibeon, known today as EL-JIB, you will see the Holy Land's best preserved water system. It is striking. Cut entirely from solid rock, it consists of a circular pool 37 feet in diameter and an incredible 82 feet deep. Take your picture of the pool so that you see the circular stairway cut out of the inside wall. The stairs have 79 steps. In addition to the pool, there is a 167-foot-long tunnel, similar to the ones at Hazor and Megiddo. It, too, is cut from solid rock and leads to a spring out-

Left: **Pool of Gibeon**

Jerusalem, but none of them is as impressive as the Sanhedrin Tombs.

From the area of these tombs you can see NABI SAMWIL, the most prominent feature of Benjamin's topography. This is the highest mountain around for about 20 miles, rising 2942 feet above sea level. It is named "Nabi Samwil," or "Nebi Samwil" because some believed that Samuel was buried here. The Bible, however, places Samuel's burial place at Ramah (I Samuel 25:1; 28:3).

Not much is left at Nabi Samwil. But the view from there provides the best view of Jerusalem in the Holy Land. It was from this site that the Christian Crusaders first viewed the Holy City on July 7, 1099, and wept for joy. The panorama of Palestine is absolutely astounding.

Some believe that this is the site of ancient MIZPEH (also spelled "Mizpah"). It was here that Samuel called Israel for prayer and rededication to Jehovah (I Samuel 7:5-7). Saul was proclaimed Israel's first king here (I Samuel 10:17-24). References to this site abound (Judges 20:1-3; I Kings 15:22; Nehemiah 3:7-19; Jeremiah 40:8; 41:10). Others hold that

GIBEON: DEATH AND VICTORY

Gibeon is where David defeated the Philistines (I Chronicles 14:16; II Samuel 5:25). Later, in an attempt to settle a dispute between the men of Abner and Joab, 12 men from each side killed each other at Gibeon's Pool (II Samuel 2:12-16). Still later, God gave King Solomon the opportunity to choose anything he wanted. He chose wisdom and an understanding heart, and God gave him riches and fame (I Kings 3:4-15; II Chronicles 1:2-17).

Perhaps the most famous biblical event that occurred at Gibeon involved both the sun and the moon. Hearing what the God of Israel did at Jericho and Ai, the Gibeonites tricked Joshua into making a league with them (Joshua 9:3-27). Subsequently, five Amorite kings joined forces against the Gibeonites. When the Israelite forces were called upon for aid, they made a forced march from Gilgal in the Jordan Valley to Gibeon in the Central Highlands. In the battle that ensued, God sent huge hailstones from heaven, which killed more of the enemy than the Israelites did. In order to complete this battle when daylight was failing him, Joshua called on the sun and moon to stand still. They miraculously obeyed and the enemy was routed (Joshua 10:1-27).

THE TOMB OF THE KINGS

These are not the tombs of the Israelite kings. They are the tombs of Queen Helena, a wealthy queen from Adiabene on the Tigris in Mesopotamia.

Having embraced Judaism, Queen Helena and her family came to Jerusalem about A.D. 45. Here she built a palace and this necropolis. An extremely wide set of 25 steps leads to a rock-hewn cistern that was used for ritual ablutions, or preparation for burial. A left turn through the archway and another left will bring you to the vestibule of the tombs. It's a room cut out of the rock, the roof of which is supported on the right by two pole braces.

Enter the vestibule and look left. There you will see the real reason why you are here. The small below-ground-level opening to the burial chamber is only about three feet high. But look at the stone. Here is a rolling stone in a small channel, or track, that was used to seal the face of the tomb. It's the very kind of stone and opening one would expect on the tomb of the Lord Jesus. This will give you an accurate and authentic representation of what a first-century A.D. tomb was like.

the city. It will be on your left, below the road. This Benjamite site (Joshua 18:28; I Samuel 13:2) was the scene of the near annihilation of the tribe of Benjamin (Judges 20:12-48). It was Saul's hometown and became his capital after his coronation as Israel's first king (I Samuel 10:26; 13:16; 15:34; Isaiah 10:29).

King Hussein of Jordan began building a palace on the ruins of Saul's fortress, but the construction was stopped abruptly in 1967, due to the Six Day War.

A bit nearer the northern outskirts of Jerusalem there is a road to the left that leads to ancient NOB. Here David received the sword of Goliath from Ahimelech the priest (I Samuel 21:1,8,9). David hid from the jealous Saul here (I Samuel 21:1,10), and in retaliation Saul killed all the priests of Nob (I Samuel 22:6-23). Several hundred yards farther up this secondary road is the site of ancient ANATHOTH, the birthplace of Jeremiah (Jeremiah 29:27). Anathoth is frequently mentioned in the Old Testament (cf. Joshua 21:17,18; I Kings 2:26; Ezra 2:23; Nehemiah 11:31,32; Isaiah 10:30; Jeremiah 1:1; 11:21-23; 29:27; 32:7-9).

As you arrive back in Jerusalem on the Nablus Road, keep your eyes open for the

side the city. Seeing Gibeon's pool is well worth the little side excursion from the Nablus Road.

If you head back toward Jerusalem, you'll pass the ruins of GIBEAH, two miles north of

American Colony Hotel on the left. Shortly thereafter the road forks. Bear left on Saladin Street. Just ahead on your left is a walled enclosure with a sign over the gate, *Tombeau Des Rois*—the TOMB OF THE KINGS.

If you're adventurous, you can enter the chamber. You will need a flashlight or candle as there is no other light source. The chamber is not very high and walking around is uncomfortable for tall people, but inside you can see 30 tombs. As you leave the chamber, make sure you see the relief carvings of grape clusters and wreaths on the walls of the rock vestibule.

If you continue south on Saladin Street toward the Old City, you'll join Sultan Suleiman Street at the Jerusalem post office. This is the street just outside the Jerusalem city wall at Herod's Gate. A block or more to the left, across from the northeastern corner of the city wall, is the ROCKEFELLER MUSEUM. Constructed by funds donated by John D. Rockefeller, Jr., and opened in 1938, the official name is the PALESTINE ARCH-AEOLOGICAL MUSEUM. The sand-white block building is easy to spot because of its octagonal tower, which rises above a garden of trees and flowers.

The main part of the museum is built around a rectangular cloister. The exhibits, which are chronologically arranged, depict the history of the Holy Land. Here you will see reliefs from Sennacherib's palace at Nineveh (c. 700 B.C.), the lintels of the Church of the Holy Sepulchre and an extensive and very impressive collection of Holy Land jewelry and coins. From the El Aksa Mosque there are intricately carved wooden panels, beams and doors. From the Caliph Hisham Palace at Jericho (eighth century A.D.) there are plaster statues of people and animals.

If you want to do some quick reading or heavy research on the Holy Land, this is the place to do it. The museum has a comfortable reading room with hundreds of periodicals and thousands of volumes, all on the subjects of Holy Land history, archaeology and geography.

THE ENVIRONS EAST

At the northeast corner of the Old City of Jerusalem you will see the Stork Tower. The Jericho Road is to the right. Straight across from the tower is a street that dips down into the Kidron Valley so sharply that it disappears out of sight. This street is "Shmuel Ben Adaya." After dipping into the valley, it climbs to the crest of the Mount of Olives. At the top you can go to the left or right.

MOUNT SCOPUS is to the left. From here you get a spectacular view of Jerusalem, one which contrasts with the stark wilderness off in the distance. Many attacks have been launched on the Holy City from Mount Scopus. The Romans under Titus in A.D. 70, the Crusaders in 1099, the British in 1917 and the Arabs in 1948 have all camped here.

The original Hadassah Hospital and the initial campus of the Hebrew University are on this mount. When this area fell within the demilitarized zone in 1948, the Jews established a new campus at Givat Ram on the west side of Jerusalem. Hadassah Hospital has also been relocated on the west side of

Opposite: The village of Nob

Below: View of the Old City from Mount Scopus

Jerusalem, near Ein Karem.

If you turn right at the head of Shmuel Ben Adaya Street, you'll reach the central heights of the MOUNT OF OLIVES. Here you'll find the RUSSIAN TOWER OF THE ASCENSION, the most noticeable structure on the mountain and the landmark with which Jerusalem is identified at a distance. Its tower rises six stories into the rarified air and is visible from miles away. The 214-step climb to the top provides a very beautiful view of the city below. According to the Russian Orthodox Church, the rock at the southeast corner of the church is the spot where Mary stood as Jesus ascended into heaven.

A nearby rival site for this honor is the CHAPEL OF THE ASCENSION, also referred to as the DOME OF ASCENSION. In A.D. 380, a round structure was built over the rock said to be the exact spot where Jesus Christ ascended. In fact, if you have a good imagination you might even see the footprint Christ supposedly left in the rock.

In 614, the Persians partially destroyed this shrine, but the Crusaders built a roofless, polygonal chapel over the rock. When the Muslims gained control of the shrine in 1187, they added the ceiling dome that is charac-

teristic of a mosque. Like so many Holy Land shrines, the site is shared by several Christian communities and denominations. On different dates different groups celebrate the Feast of Ascension here, setting up tents and portable altars. The iron hooks on the wall around the shrine mark off the areas for each community.

The PATER NOSTER CHURCH is located to the east. There in the "Our Father" church the Lord's Prayer of Matthew 6:9-15 is beautifully inscribed on 44 tiles, each in a different language. The tiles with the prayer in English, French and Hebrew are favorites with photographers. In 1868, the French Princess de la Tour d'Auvergne purchased the site and established a convent for the Carmelite Sisters. (Incidentally, the site where Jesus actually taught His disciples this prayer is in Galilee.)

Continuing to the east, you arrive in front of one the Middle East's finest hotels—the SEVEN ARCHES. Formerly the "Jerusalem Intercontinental," this hotel was built to resemble a caravansary. While not as modern as some of the newer hotels, it still carries unmatched charm and an unmatched view of Jerusalem. From the front of the hotel you will be able to see a vast Jewish cemetery which clings to

The Chapel of the Ascension

the side of the mountain. This is a favorite spot for tourists who are trying to get that once-in-a-lifetime photo of the Holy City. To add some local color (and subtract a few dollars from your wallet), the Arab entrepreneur stands ready with his camel to give you a ride. This is your only opportunity for a photo on a camel with a background of the eternal city of Jerusalem.

Few places in Palestine are as densely populated with churches as is the MOUNT OF OLIVES. More than 25 churches, chapels and convents have been built there. And why not? This mountain is considerably higher than Jerusalem and has played a central role in the city's history.

The mountain has four eminences. The northernmost and highest (2723 feet) is called Viri Galilaei because it is thought that here the angels appeared to the disciples and addressed them, "Men of Galilee, why do you stand gazing up into heaven?" (Acts 1:11). The second eminence is the site of Jesus' ascension, where the Tower of Ascension and the Muslim Dome of Ascension are located. The third eminence is where the Church of Pater Noster stands. The final one is known as the Mount of Offense—supposedly the "Mount of Corruption" where King Solomon erected the high places for the strange gods of his foreign wives (I Kings 11:1).

Just to the east of the Mount of Olives you come to BETHPHAGE. From here Jesus began His triumphal entry over the mountain and into Jerusalem (Luke 19:29-44). (The traditional road crosses the mountain at the site of the Pater Noster Church.) Jesus cursed the

HOW TO RIDE A CAMEL

Do not pass up the opportunity to ride a camel. It's not at all like riding a horse. On a horse you bounce up and down; on a camel you rock back and forth. Camels are friendly creatures, but don't try to pet their noses as you would a horse's nose. Camels have a nasty habit of spitting.

You may need some help in getting up into the box saddle. Camels are somewhat broader than horses. But once you're in the saddle and have a firm grasp on the saddle's horn, the fun begins. The camel is on his knees when you mount him. When you ride him, he will be on his feet. Back legs go up first, which means that suddenly you are thrust forward. Once the front legs are up it's like sitting on the top of the world. Coming back down is quite similar. The front legs go down to the knees; the back legs follow. You may now get off and bask in the victory of having successfully ridden a camel.

The Franciscan convent at Bethphage on the eastern slope of the Mount of Olives.
According to tradition, Jesus' triumphal entry into Jerusalem began here.

fig tree on this mount (Matthew 21:17-22; Mark 11:12-14, 20-26), and it was here that He wept over the city (Luke 19:37-44). After eating the Passover with His disciples in the Upper Room, Jesus and the Eleven went out to the Mount of Olives (Matthew 26:30; Mark 14:26; Luke 22:39).

God isn't finished with this important mountain. It figures prominently in biblical prophecy. From this very mount Jesus predicted God's judgment on the Gentile nations (Matthew 25:31-46). This judgment follows Christ's Second Coming, the Second Advent, when He comes to establish His kingdom (Joel 3:1,2). His coming to earth will actually alter the topographical structure of the Mount of Olives. The Prophet Zechariah reports, "And in that day His feet will stand on the Mount of Olives, which faces Jerusalem on the east. And the Mount of Olives shall be split in two, from east to west, making a very large valley; half of the mountain shall move toward the north and half of it toward the south" (Zechariah 14:4). A valley not in existence today will come into being when Jesus returns to the mountain from which He ascended into heaven.

As you leave the Mount of Olives and descend into the KIDRON VALLEY, you come to the most famous stream in the area—the Brook Kidron. This stream is only a wadi, a stream that is dry except when it rains. The valley and the stream gain their importance from the fact that they are immediately east of and some 400 feet below the temple area.

Over the centuries this valley has been a symbol of separation from Jerusalem and the true worship of Jehovah. For example, this is where King Asa burnt his mother's idols (I Kings 15:13; II Chronicles 15:16). And this is where Josiah destroyed the vessels of Baal that had been placed in the house of God (II Kings 23:4-6,12). King Hezekiah ordered Jerusalem's priests to carry all the "debris that they found in the temple of the Lord" and dump it in the Brook Kidron (II Chronicles 29:16). Also, during Absalom's rebellion, King David separated himself from the kingdom

The Kidron Valley, east of Jerusalem

by crossing over Kidron and seeking refuge (II Samuel 15:23).

The Valley of Kidron is also known as the Valley of Jehoshaphat. Muslims believe that Mohammed will sit by the Dome of the Rock and Jesus on the Mount of Olives. A wire will be stretched between them across which all mankind will walk. Those who have lived righteously will successfully reach the other side; those who have not will fall into the Kidron Valley and perish.

At the bottom of the Kidron Valley road—which is also the Jericho Road—there is a sharp "S" curve. To your left, as you negotiate the curve, you will find the GARDEN OF GETHSEMANE. The name means "wine" or "oil press." Your visit to the garden will show you why. The Garden is maintained by the Franciscans and contains eight severely gnarled olive trees, believed to date from the first century. This beautifully maintained garden is undoubtedly much better manicured than it was in the days of our Lord. In fact, the Russian Gethsemane, higher on the hill than the Latin garden, is probably much more like the one Jesus visited. Nonetheless, if you stand at just the right place, you have a great opportunity to take a picture of the Jerusalem wall and the Golden (Eastern) Gate framed by twisted and ancient olive trees. The scene makes an ideal picture.

The BASILICA OF THE AGONY is adjacent

to this restful garden of prayer. This Roman Catholic church is constructed in Byzantine style and was dedicated by the Franciscans in 1924. Since it was built by funds donated from all over the world, it is also known as the CHURCH OF ALL NATIONS. There is an impressive facade above three gigantic arches on the front side of the church. The colorful mosaic depicts Jesus weeping over the city in Gethsemane. The church itself features six huge pillars that support a roof of 12 white domes. If you view the church from the Mount of Olives above, you will see that it resembles a somewhat ornate box of table tennis balls.

The church is extremely dark inside. The windows are made of translucent alabaster; and they yield only soft, mysterious light.

Straight ahead you will see an area encircled by a wrought-iron fence that reminds you of thorns. Within this fence a huge rock projects through the mosaic floor of the church. The rock, which measures approximately 25 feet square, is reported to be the site where Jesus prayed in agony in the garden (Luke 22:39-46) before His crucifixion. Above the rock is a scene of mosaic that depicts Jesus kneeling in prayer in Gethsemane. Since admittance to the olive-treed garden outside is prohibited, the many wooden benches in the basilica, facing the lighted rock of agony, provide an excellent opportunity to spend time in prayer.

Perhaps the most unusual church in the Holy Land, architecturally speaking, is located on the mountain above the basilica—the RUSSIAN ORTHODOX CHURCH OF MARY

View of the Eastern Gate from Gethsemane

MAGDALENE. The seven golden, onion-shaped domes, or spires, on the church gracefully rise out of a garden of olive trees. Built in 1888 by Alexander III, Czar of Russia, in memory of his mother, the church is maintained by the White Russian nuns. It is the Russian Gethsemane.

South of this unique church and a bit farther up the side of the mountain you will see a small, single-domed church. It is known as DOMINUS FLEVIT, which means "the Lord wept." According to tradition, this marks the spot where Jesus stopped to weep over Jerusalem as He was coming from Bethphage on an ass (Luke 19:29,41-44). The roof of the church looks like an inverted tulip but was actually designed to suggest a tear drop. The four corners of the roof are styled to resemble tear bottles. This Byzantine chapel features an austere altar backed by a glass window that provides a panoramic view of the temple area.

If you follow the main road from the Garden of Gethsemane toward Jericho, in a minute or two you'll round another "S" curve and arrive at the CHURCH OF SAINT LAZARUS. Climb the pathway through the garden, and you arrive at the courtyard outside the church. To your left is the Franciscan Church, which was built in 1953 and dedicated to Lazarus. The church is decorated with mosaics that depict the events that took place in Bethany, and it incorporates the fourth-century ruins of the first shrine on the site. To your right

The Garden of Gethsemane and the Church of All Nations

JESUS IN GETHSEMANE

Somewhere on the side of this mountain, across the Kidron Valley from Jerusalem's Golden Gate (Luke 22:39,40), Jesus often came to pray. Here He met with His disciples and prayed with them (John 18:2).

On one particular night, however, He agonized in prayer with an exceedingly sorrowful soul (Matthew 26:36-38). And to this place Judas led a band of men and officers sent from the chief priests and Pharisees. That night Judas betrayed the Lord (John 18:1-13). Here the ever impetuous Peter drew his sword and sliced off the right ear of a servant of the High Priest (v.10). Jesus Christ was arrested, bound and dragged away before the high priest (vv. 12,13). In the quietness of the Garden of Gethsemane, we can imagine the clamor as they took Him away.

Lilies in the Garden of Gethsemane

and adjacent to the tomb, you will see a sixteenth-century mosque. Ahead you will also see a Greek Orthodox Church and the remains of a fortified Crusader tower.

After you visit the church, be sure to see the remains of a grain mill and a spectacular olive press. Go across the courtyard and through the door of the 2000-year-old home; then turn right. There, in a darkened room, you will see the press, which has a huge stone, a wooden beam and a turn screw.

Outside the church complex and a bit farther up the hill, on the left side of the road, you will come to the traditional TOMB OF LAZARUS. The walk to the tomb will take less than a minute. The smallish opening to the tomb is only four square stones high, and it has a huge stone lintel over the door. Above the entrance a large blue sign marks the site. If you enter the tomb, you can take the 27 slippery steps down and enter a burial chamber. Whether or not this is actually Lazarus' tomb is doubtful (John 11:1-44).

Across the steep road from the Tomb of Lazarus you will find a souvenir shop. One of the shopkeepers will cheerfully demonstrate his keen ability with a slingshot, the kind used by David. He will use his little stringed pouch to hurl a stone hundreds of feet into the air. While we stand amazed at his ability, he points in the direction he has hurled the stone and asks, "Do you know who's there?" "Who?" you ask. "My mother-in-law" comes the reply.

This shop is a great place to buy olive-oil soap. The two-inch square bars have an amazing effect on people who have rough hands or dry skin.

The village of BETHANY was once the home of Mary, Martha and Lazarus (John 11:1), as well as of Simon the leper (Mark 14:3). Our Lord made this town His Judaean "home" (Matthew 21:17; Mark 11:11). At the home of Mary and Martha, Mary sat at Jesus' feet in adoration as Martha scurried around, serving the disciples (Luke 10:38-42). At the house of Simon the leper, Judas Iscariot complained about the waste when Mary anointed Jesus

with a spikenard of precious oil (Matthew 26:6-13; Mark 14:3-9; John 12:1-8).

As you return to the Kidron Valley, along the Mount of Olives, you may reflect on the time that Jesus cursed a barren fig tree as he was returning from Bethany one morning (Matthew 21:17-22; Mark 11:12-14). As you leave Bethany, take the Jericho Road until you get to the Silwan Road. Then turn left. This road descends into the Kidron Valley and leads you to SILWAN.

Silwan is an Arab village, layered on the slopes of the southeast corner of Jerusalem's Old City. Along the left side of the road are four of the oddest-looking structures in the Holy Land. They are distinctively shaped tombs, each with a unique style of architecture and an unusual story.

The first tomb is the PILLAR OF ABSALOM, or the Tomb of Absalom. The tomb is a monolithic cube with a circular cap that rises to a balled point. Hellenistic in design, it is cut entirely out of the rock and stands 60 feet high. Tradition ascribes this tomb to Absalom, David's wayward son. Some have thought it might even be the pillar Absalom built for himself "in the King's Valley" (II Samuel 18:17,18). However, it was probably

erected 700 years later, during the period of the Second Temple. Inside the pillar is a rock-hewn burial chamber.

The TOMB OF JEHOSHAPHAT is behind this pillar and almost entirely hidden by it. Cut out of the same rock as the pillar, this tomb is an alcove with eight burial chambers inside. The entrance is ornately carved in mixed Graeco-Egyptian style and features a frieze of acanthus leaves.

The BENI HEZIR TOMBS are next. Carved into the face of the rock is a Hasmonean portico. Above four Doric columns of this facade is a Hebrew inscription indicating that these were the burial chambers of a Herodian priestly family of the Sons of Hezir, "Beni Hezir" (Nehemiah 10:20). This is the oldest of the four tombs, dating from the Hasmonean period (second century B.C.).

An old Hebrew tradition claims that it was here that King Uzziah (Azariah) isolated him-

self when he had leprosy (II Kings 15:5). According to a Christian tradition, this site was associated with Jesus' cousin, James. In the fourth century, monks found a skeleton here which they claimed to be that of James. In the sixth century a tradition arose that James hid here after Jesus' arrest. By the fifteenth century the tradition had grown to identify this as James' actual tomb.

The final tomb, and the most recent, is the TOMB OF ZECHARIAH. It is a solid rock cube with four pillars carved on the front and with a pyramid top. This first-century tomb is believed to be that of the Hebrew prophet Zechariah. However, many Christians believe this to be the tomb of Zacharias, the father of John the Baptist. A tunnel from beneath the tomb leads to the tombs of Beni Hezir.

It is possible that Jesus was referring to one or all of these tombs when He alluded to the hypocritical Pharisees as being like whited sepulchres, beautiful on the outside but filthy and dead inside (Matthew 23:27).

THE ENVIRONS SOUTH

Entrance to Hezekiah's Tunnel

Just beyond the Pinnacle of the Temple, the southeast corner of the Old City wall,

the Silwan Road enters the village of Silwan, or Siloam. To your right is the GIHON SPRING, one of Jerusalem's earliest sources of water. About 3000 years ago the Jebusite inhabitants of Jerusalem dug an underground waterway to this bubbling stream. This was the "water shaft" the men of David used to stealthily enter the city and capture it (II Samuel 5:6-10). As a result, Jerusalem became the "City of David" and his political, religious and military capital. Later, the Gihon Spring was the site of Solomon's coronation as Israel's third king (I Kings 1:33-45).

The Gihon Spring is also known as the FOUNTAIN OF THE VIRGIN because of a fourteenth-century legend that Mary washed Jesus' clothes in this spring. To enter, you must descend a set of 33 stone steps to a grilled entrance. Here is the beginning of the Holy Land's most famous tunnel, HEZEKIAH'S TUNNEL (II Kings 20:20; II Chronicles 32:2-4; Isaiah 36,37).

Because the Gihon Spring was outside the city wall, it was always vulnerable to enemy attack. In 701 B.C., the Assyrian King Sennacherib invaded Palestine and threatened Jerusalem (II Kings 18:17-21). In order to secure the city's water source, King Hezekiah had a conduit chiseled out of the subterranean rock of the HILL OPHEL, the southern ridge of Mount Moriah. At the end of this conduit and within the walls of the Lower City, he built a reservoir for his tunnel, the POOL OF SILOAM. When the Gihon Spring was covered and camouflaged, the city would have ample water for the entire siege.

Although the distance between the Gihon Spring and the Pool of Siloam is only 1090 feet, the tunnel zigs and zags its way for 1770 feet through the solid rock. What is really remarkable is that Hezekiah's workmen began at both ends and cut toward the center. The account of this engineering feat was engraved in the stone wall. In 1880 a young boy discovered this inscription in ancient Hebrew script some 19 feet from the Siloam end of the conduit. Ten years later, unfortunately, it was moved to the Istanbul Museum.

The tunnel averages a little more than two feet wide and six feet high. The floor is slippery and rocky because of the constant flow of water. When I last waded through the tunnel, the water was high, up to my shoulders in places. But if the waters are not unusually high, and if you don't mind getting wet, you can take a refreshing stroll through one of Jerusalem's oldest antiquities, one that has remained almost undisturbed since 700 B.C.

A fifth-century church was built over the Pool of Siloam, but it was destroyed by the Persians in A.D. 614 and never rebuilt. All that remains today is a relatively deep, walled hole in the ground. Stone steps lead down to the crystal-clear waters that flow from the round exit of Hezekiah's Tunnel. You can also see the remains of a Roman bath in these waters. Above the ground is a small mosque with a slender minaret rising toward the skies from a grove of trees.

This pool is probably the same as "the Pool of Shelah by the King's Garden" (Nehemiah 3:15) and "the waters of Shiloah that go softly" (Isaiah 8:6). Luke 13:4 records that once a tower fell at this pool and killed 18 people. It was at this pool that the blind man was instructed by Jesus to wash after our Lord spat on the ground and applied the soft clay to his eyes. The man's sight returned and he was taken to the Pharisees. An inane discussion followed as to whether or not Jesus was a sinner for healing him on the Sabbath. The man's answer was a classic: "Whether He is a sinner or not I do not know. One thing I know: that though I was blind, now I see" (John 9:1-25). We should not attempt to explain God's gifts to us, whether they be sight or salvation. Rather, we ought to accept them and enjoy them.

Farther down the Silwan Road, and on the same side, is the infamous potter's field known

The Pool of Siloam

Above: Aceldama—where Judas hung himself

Right: Solomon's Pools

as HACELDAMA (also spelled without an "H" and sometimes spelled "Hakeldema"). The name means "field of blood." After Judas betrayed Jesus for 30 pieces of silver and began to feel uncomfortable about it, he returned to the temple and cast the silver at the feet of the priests. After Judas killed himself, this money was used to buy a plot in the potter's field in which to bury strangers (Matthew 27:1-10). This event corresponds exactly to the prophecy of Zechariah 11:12,13.

Today the GREEK ORTHODOX CONVENT OF SAINT ONIPRIUS marks this site, and it is set among Jewish burial caves of the Second Temple period (about 450 B.C. to A.D. 70). These caves have also been known as the APOSTLES' CAVES, because they were reported to be the hiding places of the apostles during Jesus' trial. They are filled with skulls and bones.

Nestled in the Judaean hills just a few miles south of Jerusalem, Bethlehem, at 2350 feet above sea level, is several hundred feet lower than the capital. As you approach the town on the road from Jerusalem, the road forks just past Rachel's Tomb. To the right, the road skirts the west side of Bethlehem and continues on to Hebron. About two miles south of town are three large reservoirs known as SOLOMON'S POOLS. These reservoirs supplied Jerusalem and Bethlehem with water

through a conduit. Although Solomon's pools are mentioned in Ecclesiastes 2:4-6, these reservoirs are probably misnamed, since two of them were built by Pontius Pilate and the third in the fifteenth century.

The left fork of the road is Manger Street. This snakes its way upward toward Bethlehem, past the Holy Land Christian Mission, Saint Joseph's Church and King David's Wells. At the end of Manger Street a sharp right turn at the top of the hill brings you directly into the center of MANGER SQUARE. Here tens of thousands of Christian pilgrims gather each Christmas Eve to celebrate the birth of Jesus Christ.

Souvenir shops edge the square on several sides. Here, too, is St. George's, one of my favorite restaurants. It serves local Arab food, and the pita bread is absolutely the best in the world!

On the east side of the square is the main attraction of Bethlehem, the CHURCH OF THE NATIVITY. It is a large building that looks like a fort. Its high gray walls extend all the way to the square on the right side. Its bell towers are on its right extension; on its left is a fenced garden. Outwardly it seems cold and unfriendly.

The door of the church is narrow and low, allowing only one person at a time to enter. Tradition says that the less-than-four-foot-high door was constructed to cause all who enter to bow before the sacred spot. Another tradition holds that the Crusaders

"O LITTLE TOWN OF BETHLEHEM"

For the Christian pilgrim the main attraction in the environs south of Jerusalem is BETHLEHEM. With the exception of Jerusalem, Bethlehem is the most important city in Christendom. Immortalized in song and poetry, this picturesque village lays claim to prominence in both the Old and New Testaments.

Bethlehem ("house of bread") is first mentioned in the Bible as the place where Rachel died giving birth to Benjamin (Genesis 35:16-20). Jacob marked her tomb with a memorial pillar. First Samuel 10:2 places this sepulcher "in the territory of Benjamin at Zelzah." About one mile north of Bethlehem, on the right side of the road from Jerusalem, you will see the traditional site of RACHEL'S TOMB. The 23-foot-square shrine has been rebuilt several times, the last time in 1841 by Sir Moses Montefiore. It looks strikingly like a small mosque, with a white cupola crowning the square shrine. Israeli soldiers are always on the rooftop across the street, monitoring the traffic entering Bethlehem and watching Rachel's tomb, because it is sacred—to Jews, Muslims and Christians alike.

Bethlehem was the home and burial place of Ibzan, the tenth judge in Israel (Judges 12:8-10). The Levite's concubine who was abused while sojourning in the mountain of Ephraim was from Bethlehem of Judea (Judges 19).

The Book of Ruth is staged here. Elimelech and Naomi left Bethlehem of Judea to sojourn in Moab during a severe famine. When Naomi and her daughter-in-law Ruth returned to the Holy Land, they came back to Bethlehem. It was in the fields on the outskirts of this village that the beautiful romance between Ruth and Boaz blossomed. Ruth became the great grandmother of David (Ruth 4:17; I Samuel 17:12). Thus, Bethlehem is the "City of David" and the home of the Davidic family. Samuel came to Bethlehem to anoint the shepherd boy David as king of Israel (I Samuel 16:4,11-13). On the terraced slopes and grass-covered fields of Bethlehem, you can still see shepherd boys tending their flocks much the same way young David once did (I Samuel 17:15).

But the great biblical importance of Bethlehem is the village's link with David's great descendant, Jesus Christ the Lord. The prophet Micah pinpoints Bethlehem Ephratah, "little among the thousands of Judah," as the birthplace of Israel's Messiah and the world's Redeemer (Micah 5:2). Micah's prophecy was fulfilled (Luke 2:4-7), and the shepherds came from the nearby fields to adore the Christchild (Luke 2:15,16). Later, Herod the Great, when he learned that the wise men came to seek the King of the Jews, slaughtered "all the male children who were in Bethlehem and in all its districts, from two years old and under" (Matthew 2:15-18). But an angel of the Lord had already appeared to Joseph, and he fled with Mary and the baby Jesus to Egypt (Matthew 2:13-23; Jeremiah 31:15; 40:1).

Rachel's Tomb

constructed the door low in order to keep marauders from desecrating the church by riding in and out on horseback. Once you are inside, the fortress appearance of the church suddenly disappears.

The Church of the Nativity is Christianity's oldest church still in use. A grotto beneath the church was identified as the birthplace of Jesus by Helena, mother of Constantine, in A.D. 325. Shortly thereafter the Emperor constructed a church at this site. The present building was built by the Roman Emperor Justinian (A.D. 527-565), who intended this edifice to be one of the finest churches in his extensive empire. This was the only church in the Holy Land that was not destroyed by the Persians in 614. It was completely altered, however, by the Crusaders, and its interior is a splendid example of a beautiful basilica of the Byzantine period.

The church is 170 feet long and 80 feet wide. It is divided into five naves by four rows of rose-brown Corinthian pillars made of the red stone of the country. To your left there are double rows of pillars with 12 columns in a row. To your right is the same. Each pillar bears a faint picture of an apostle. The floor is constructed of square, stone blocks. At several locations on the left side, wooden trapdoors can be raised to expose the original mosaic floor beneath. This floor was discovered in 1936.

Look up at the ceiling. Oak rafters grace it much the same way in which rafters give a quiet elegance to any old building. The rest of the church is overly ornate. Hanging on long chains from this simple ceiling are several dozen gilded lamp fixtures that resemble fancy kerosene lamps. Make your way to the front of the church to see the ICONOSTASIS, the beautifully carved wall that separates the altar from the holy place of the church.

You must ascend several steps to get to the ALTAR OF THE NATIVITY. Hanging from the ceiling in the center is a magnificent gold and silver chandelier. Silver and gold abound, but the face of the altar, in typical drab-dark orthodox decor, is made of hand-carved cedars from Lebanon. The area to the left of the altar is under the jurisdiction of the Armenian Church. The area to the right is the domain of the Greek Orthodox Church. Franciscan priests can also be seen tending to the needs of the basilica.

You can easily identify these three different orders. The Greeks dress in long black robes; they are bearded and they wear their long black hair tied in a bun at the back. The Franciscans dress modestly in simple brown robes, usually with a cord tied at the waist. The Armenians are far more colorful in their purple and cream-colored robes. They are

easy to identify as they scurry through the church.

On both sides of the altar there are stone steps that disappear into the floor of the church. You can spot them quickly; they are just off the altar area to the back and are usually guarded by a priest with outstretched offering plate. Descend through the right side, as the traffic flows in one direction.

When you reach the bottom of the half-dozen or so steps, you enter the doorway of a cave under the altar. This is the GROTTO OF THE NATIVITY, the traditional site of the Bethlehem manger, where Jesus was born. If you come to the Holy Land expecting to find a manger filled with hay, a few lowing cattle and a rustic reminder of Christ's birth, you'll be disappointed in what you see. What you'll find is a narrow room (35 x 10 feet) in a cave, with two sacred spots and enough incense in the air to make your eyes water. To your left is the place where Mary took the Christ-child, "wrapped Him in swaddling clothes, and laid Him in a manger" (Luke 2:7). To the right is the place where the virgin gave birth to our Lord.

As you face the tiny grotto in the wall of this cave, you see a number of incense burners hanging above a silver star that marks the site of Christ's birth. This 14-pointed star has at its center an eternal flame and this inscription in Latin: "Here of the Virgin Mary, Christ was born."

The cave itself is dark; the primitive rock of the cave is blackened by the smoke of the candles, oil lamps and incense. The walls of the grotto are covered with asbestos to protect against fire. But that won't dampen your spirits or the reverence with which you and other Christians regard this place. You may even want to sing a Christmas carol or two before you leave.

As you exit up the stairs into the Armenian quarter of the basilica, you will go through a nearby door into an adjacent chapel. To your immediate right is a stairway that descends through the floor next to the wall. This stairway leads into another cave, and the

CHAPEL OF SAINT JEROME. It was in this subterranean monastery that the great biblical scholar Jerome sequestered himself during the last 35 years of his life (A.D. 386-420) meditating, studying, writing and translating. It was here that he translated the Bible from Hebrew and Greek into Latin. His translation is the famous Latin Vulgate.

If you go back up the stairs and out the rear doors, you will enter a courtyard of cloisters where you'll see a statue of Jerome (spelled "Hieronymus") on a high column. Once outside the courtyard, make your way left through

Jesus' traditional birthplace

Shepherds' Fields near Bethlehem

the gardens to the stone-faced courtyard and then back to Manger Square.

From the square you can take Shepherds' Street past the Terra Sancta College to Beit Sahur, a tiny Arab village. Just beyond it, east of Bethlehem, you will see SHEPHERDS' FIELD. "Now there were in the same country shepherds living out in the fields, keeping watch over their flock by night" (Luke 2:8). In this pastoral setting, you can almost relive the eventful night. "When the fullness of the time had come, God sent forth his Son, born of a woman, born under the law, to redeem those who were under the law, that we might receive the adoption as sons" (Galatians 4:4,5). As you stand under the starry hosts and as you see the hillsides terraced with olive trees and fields glowing with golden grain, you may think it ironic that the Son of God became a man so that men might become the sons of God. All babes are born to live; this One was born to die.

Listen carefully. Perhaps you can still hear the angels sing: "Hail the heav'n born Prince of Peace, Hail the Sun of righteousness! Light and life to all He brings, Ris'n with healing in His wings; Mild He lays His glory by, Born that man no more may die; Born to raise the sons of earth, Born to give them second birth. Hark! the herald angels sing, 'Glory to the newborn King.'"

MAR SABA

The MAR SABA MONASTERY is located about nine miles east of Bethlehem on a narrow, lonely road in the Judean wilderness. Founded in the fifth century by the monk Saba and named after him ("mar" means holy), the monastery is inhabited by only a handful of monks today. It is the most spectacular of all the desert monasteries, consisting of many structures that seem to be piled on top of one another behind a high, fortress-like wall. Many paintings grace the walls of this simple monastery. The dining area is the most spartan of all the rooms.

The skeleton of Saba lies entombed in a glass coffin in the main cathedral. The skulls of all the monks who have served and died here are placed in glass cabinets and are visible to all. The present structure was built by the Russians in the nineteenth century. While women may look into the compound from the seventeenth-century watchtower called the Women's Tower, no woman is ever permitted to enter the monastery.

The site is eerie. The monastery is perched high above the Kidron Valley. (This valley, which is situated between the Temple Mount and the Mount of Olives, continues through the wilderness here and on to the Dead Sea.) The view down into the deep ravine is lovely, but finding civilization this far into the sandy, barren wilderness is a bit spooky.

THE ENVIRONS WEST

The main gate leading west from the Old City is the Jaffa Gate. If you drive west from this gate, you'll come almost immediately to Jerusalem's grandest park, Independence Park. Turn left on Agron Street and you will be on one of the main thoroughfares that cut across Jerusalem. Follow it until it intersects King George Street. At the corner is HECHAL SHLOMO, the imposing Seat of the Rabbinate, the supreme religious center of Judaism. This building is styled along the lines of King Solomon's Temple. ("Hechel Shlomo" means "palace or temple of Solomon.") It is square at the bottom with a rounded top. Inside is a synagogue, a library, a museum, the Abraham Wax Collection of Jewish Religions and an interesting series of dioramas depicting biblical events. Here you may purchase some authentic Jewish souvenirs.

Next door to Hechal Schlomo is the JERUSALEM GREAT SYNAGOGUE. This multi-storied synagogue is believed by some Christians to be an interim step in the construction of the future Jerusalem Temple. But anyone who visits this synagogue will come away a bit disappointed if they expected anything approaching Solomon's temple.

Outside, Agron Street becomes Ramban Street and continues west to the KNESSET, Israel's Parliament. The supreme legislative body of the State of Israel, the Knesset is a single-chambered house of 120 members,

A VISIT TO BETHLEHEM

Do not plan to spend Christmas Eve in Bethlehem unless you have made special arrangements with the Israel Government Tourist Offices (I.G.T.O.) in Jerusalem, Tel Aviv or Haifa. If you have a guide, he can do this for you.

Because thousands of pilgrims will jam Manger Square, and because many thousands more will be turned away, admission to the Square on Christmas Eve is restricted only to tourists holding special tickets. You may find the overwhelming crowds, the noticeable presence of the Israeli military and the inclement weather sufficient reason for planning some alternative form of Christmas Eve observance.

Bethlehem has become one of the shopping capitals of Israel, especially for tourists. On the way into town you will pass many fine shops with shopkeepers eager to serve you. These shops are equally prevalent around Manger Square. Bethlehem is the place to buy world-famous olive-wood items, like carvings, plaques and figurines. Mother-of-pearl items, such as pins and brooches, are particularly nice. If you really want to please your friends, buy next year's Christmas cards in Bethlehem. You will be overwhelmed at what you can buy in the shops. You may be overwhelmed at the prices as well. But my theory of foreign purchases is: "If you can't buy it at home, it's not expensive here!"

Above: **The Knesset**

Below: **Jerusalem Menorah**

reception hall, a synagogue, a complex of meeting chambers, exhibition halls, offices, lounges, press galleries and separate kitchens for meat and milk dishes (Kosher, you know). The Knesset has a fine library of more than 80,000 volumes. If you arrive at the Knesset on Monday, Tuesday or Wednesday afternoons, you can attend a session of the Parliament. Tour groups can view the buildings on Sunday and Thursday.

Across the street from the entrance to the Knesset is the 16-foot-high MENORAH. Carved by the British sculptor Benno Elkan, the 29 panels on this seven-branched candlestick depict scenes from Jewish history. A gift from the British Parliament, the menorah is the symbol of the State of Israel. Although it is more than twice as tall as a man, it makes a good backdrop for a photo.

elected every four years in a general election. One of several government buildings in a complex, the seven-million-dollar Knesset building is made of peach/pink native Jerusalem stone. It resembles a four-story building flattened to one story. This elegant political landmark is perched on the highest hill on Jerusalem's West Side. It features a 24-foot high mosaic by Marc Chagall in the

If you take Ruppin Road across the shallow Valley of the Cross, you'll arrive at the ISRAEL MUSEUM. This complex includes the Betzelel Museum of Art and Folklore and the Bronfman Archaeological and Antiquities Museum, all set in the Billy Rose Art Garden.

The most famous and important section of the complex is the SHRINE OF THE BOOK. Above ground the museum consists of a white dome (resembling a huge Hershey's kiss), made of 275,000 glazed bricks and a black basalt rectangular block. Beneath is the museum that houses the world-famous Dead Sea Scrolls. The white dome and contrasting black block are symbolic of the conflict between light and darkness, good and evil. The Essenes, a brotherhood of Jewish ascetics who lived at Qumran on the northwest corner of the Dead Sea and copied the Dead Sea Scrolls, penned one document known as the Sons of Light and the Sons of Darkness. The museum reflects the theme of the apocalyptic scroll.

Make your way down the flight of outside stairs to the subterranean entrance of the museum. This whole unique structure exhibits a series of symbols. The entranceway is a tunnel-like passage with glass-faced niches on both sides featuring letter fragments, household items and pieces of clothing. The main hall of the museum, under the white dome, is designed to symbolize a cave. All the time you are in the Shrine of the Book you have the feeling that you are underground, perhaps in one of the Qumran caves.

Many interesting items can be seen on the two levels of the museum. There are keys, locks, coins and even a marriage contract dated April 5, A.D.128. Along the perimeter of the museum, you can peer into the walls and see fragments of the Leviticus, Psalms and Isaiah scrolls in specially treated display areas. In the center of the museum, on the upper level, you can see a large replica of a scroll handle rising from a cylinder. A copy of the great Isaiah Scroll found in Cave One is stretched around the cylinders. This is the central feature of the museum. Artifacts and letters from the Bar Kochba years are also on display on the lower level.

As you exit the museum, you will find a fine bookstore to your right. Books on the scrolls, color slides, posters and other souvenirs can be purchased. It's worth a stop.

From the Israel Museum, proceed southwest on Rav Herzog Street to the Holyland Hotel. Behind the hotel is a most interesting MODEL OF ANCIENT JERUSALEM. Commissioned by the owner of the hotel in memory of a son, the model took seven years to construct.

A team of architects, archaeologists and historians were led by noted Hebrew University archaeologist Professor Michael Avi-Yonah in planning and producing the model. On a scale of 1:50 (One-fourth inch equals one foot), this is a nearly perfect model of the Second Temple period (A.D. 66)—Herod's Jerusalem. Opulent palaces, mammoth walls, splendid public buildings, massive fortifications, private dwellings and the magnificent Second Temple itself have all been modeled. Wherever possible, the original materials of cut stone, marble, iron, wood and copper have been used.

The model covers a quarter of an acre, and it places many of the present historic remains

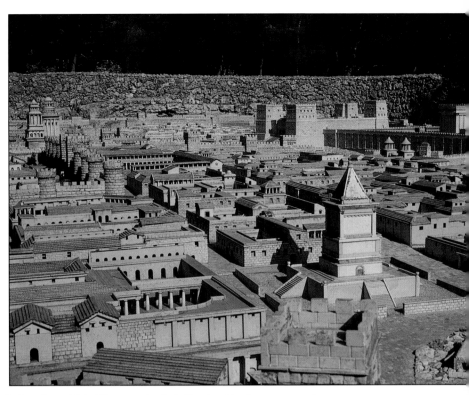

Model of Herod's Jerusalem

in the Old City and vicinity in their proper perspective. Taking a walk around its perimeter is an excellent way to become oriented to what Jerusalem must have looked like to our Lord. This is a "must see" site.

Then you take the highway that runs past the model northward. As it bends, you can see a world-renowned institution to your left, the HADASSAH HOSPITAL. This vast complex rises 12 stories from the top of a mountain above the village of Ein Karem. The hospital was originally established on Mount Scopus, on the opposite side of Jerusalem. But it became inaccessible after the War of Independence when Mount Scopus fell within the demilitarized zone. The new Hadassah was opened in 1961.

The $30-million Hadassah Hebrew University Medical Center is the largest medical center in the Middle East. It contains an 800-bed hospital, a family and community center and a child guidance clinic, as well as a medical school. More than 2000 students of medicine, dentistry, pharmacy, public health, bacteriology and nursing are served by these impressive facilities.

To the left of the main entrance of the

Above: The Church of the Visitation commemorates the meeting of Mary and Elizabeth.

Right: Tower of the Church of the Visitation

gin Mary to Elizabeth. The small mosque crowns the rock from which the town spring bubbles forth.

Farther west along the hillside is the CHURCH OF THE VISITATION. This Franciscan church is best reached by climbing the stairway from the Russian Compound. The street leads to an ornate wrought-iron gate. The facade of the church is a bright mosaic, with a scene portraying Mary's visit to the town. Inside is a grotto marking the site where it is believed that John was hidden during the

Hadassah Hospital is a small synagogue which exhibits the world-famous stained-glass windows by Marc Chagall. Each window is an abstract masterpiece depicting the 12 tribes of Israel. Viewing these magnificent windows makes the trip to the hospital worthwhile.

Beyond the hospital is a junction. The main road continues north. A second road turns left toward the Yad Vashem Memorial. A third road slices back sharply to your left and winds into the village of EIN KAREM.

Nestled enchantingly on a terraced hillside amid tall cypress trees and olive groves, Ein Karem is the birthplace of John the Baptist. It is also the scene of Mary's visit to Elizabeth, John's mother.

North of the center of town, against the terraced hills, is SAINT JOHN'S CHURCH. The present church dates from 1675 and is built over the grotto thought to be the birthplace of John the Baptist. The main altar of the church is dedicated to John; a secondary altar, off to the right, is dedicated to Elizabeth. To the left of the nave is a small stairway that leads down to the grotto. Under the marble altar is a small niche said to be John's birthplace.

Just south of the main road through Ein Karem and at the bottom of the hill is the SPRING OF THE VINEYARD (Ein Karem) MOSQUE. Since Crusader times this spring has been associated with the visit of the vir-

murder of innocent children by the jealous Herod (Matthew 2:16).

To see the rest of the church, you must return to the entrance courtyard and ascend the stairs to the east. These lead from the lower church to the upper church. Here you can see some of the finest floor mosaics of Holy Land flora and fauna. There are also attractive frescoes on the walls portraying scenes from Mary's life. Plaques in several languages reveal the text of the Magnificat (Luke 1:46-55).

Go back to the junction and take the road that leads to YAD VASHEM. (You will skirt Mount Herzl and the magnificent Herzl Tomb along the way.) The street that leads to this memorial is called the AVENUE OF THE RIGHTEOUS. The trees that line both sides of this avenue were planted by Gentiles who risked their lives in assisting the escape of Jews from the Nazis.

On top of this hill is a complex of memorials. None is as moving, as frightening, as solemn or as unforgettable as the Yad Vashem Memorial. Dedicated to the memory of the six million Jews slaughtered by the Nazis during World War II, this memorial also houses the Documentation and Research Centre. This center contains tens of thousands of pieces of microfilm relating to the Holocaust. The heavy gate at the entrance is an abstract tapestry of twisted and jagged steel, designed by David Polombo to symbolize pain, agony and anguish. You can almost feel the suffering of the six million Jews as you peer through the gate.

The memorial itself is a plain rectangular building, sad and simple. The lower portion is constructed of rounded unhewn boulders. Inside is a huge crypt-like room where a flickering eternal flame casts an otherworldly light on a mosaic floor in which is inscribed the names of the 21 largest concentration camps in which Jews lost their lives. No one can visit Yad Vashem and remain emotionally untouched.

From this solemn hill, return to the main road heading north—Herzl Boulevard. Fol-

low this all the way around New Jerusalem until it becomes Yirmiyahu Street at the extreme northwest corner of Jerusalem's environs. A left turn onto Brandeis Street brings you to one of Jerusalem's most delightful spots—the BIBLICAL ZOO. Professor Aaron Shulov of the Hebrew University's Biology Department has gathered into this unique zoo almost all of the 100 animals and

Above: **Monument at the Holocaust Museum**

Below: **Yad Vashem Memorial**

Hebrew inscriptions on tombs: מרת רעכל ראטה ע"ה and ר' יהושע בריאון ז"ל

The Jewish cemetery overlooking Jerusalem

30 birds mentioned in the Bible. With each bird or animal there is a plaque citing the book, chapter and verse in which the animal is mentioned.

The zoo was founded in 1939 on Mount Scopus. When the War of Independence broke out in 1948, there were 122 animals in the zoo. But when Mount Scopus fell into the demilitarized zone after the war, an armored convoy brought the 18 animals that survived the war to this present location. This site in the Schneller woods is a shaded glen with tall cypress and fir trees all around. By 1967, the animal population had grown to 500. However, 110 animals fell victim to the fighting of the Six Day War. Since then, the zoo has been expanding steadily.

Return to Brandeis Street and retrace your steps. Cross Yirmiyahu and continue to Malchei Israel. Turn left on this street and drive until it becomes Mea Shearim Street. Here you enter a unique quarter of Jerusalem. It is exotic and extreme, delightful and distressing, fascinating and frightening. It's like stepping out of the Middle East and into Medieval Europe. It is MEA SHEARIM, the super orthodox quarter of northwestern Jerusalem.

"Mea Shearim" is said to be derived from Genesis 26:12: "Then Isaac sowed in that land, and reaped in the same year a hundredfold [Mea Shearim]; and the LORD blessed him." This quarter was one of the earliest settlements outside the Old City and was built with a 100-gate wall as a defense against Arab marauders. Within this quarter, time has stopped. The cobblestone streets and lanes are lined with dingy houses with shuttered windows. Since 1887, Mea Shearim has been a bastion for the pious, a hotbed of Jewish orthodoxy.

The quarter is the center of the mystical Hasidic religious sect and is inhabited by descendants and immigrants from the Russian and Polish ghettos. They are orthodox Jews and dress in a distinct garb. You will recognize them immediately. The bearded men trudge through the winding streets in black gowns, wearing the beaver fur hat of the Hasidic sects or else the black wide-brimmed felt hat of other orthodox sects. The boys wear short pants with long black socks. Long, curly sidelocks fall beneath the black hats of both the men and boys. The women dress with extreme modesty, wearing long dresses and covering their shoulders and arms. Their heads are always covered. In fact, when you enter Mea Shearim, you are greeted with signs warning you that women dressed immodestly (by Hasidic standards) are not welcome.

This is a highly religious place. Scribes painstakingly copy the Scriptures by hand. Every other building is either a synagogue, a theological institution (yeshivot) or a seminar school (midrashim). Hundreds of tiny sects live here, each with its own revered rabbi and private synagogue.

There is no automobile traffic or movement on the Sabbath. However, late on the Sabbath night, the faithful make their way to the Western Wall to offer prayers. Here is a living remnant of the Jewish orthodox faith that once was so common but is now confined to a pious parcel of Palestine known as Mea Shearim. Visiting this quarter is an experience you won't soon forget.

CHAPTER ELEVEN

DESTINY'S CITY

JERUSALEM

"Great is the LORD, and greatly to be praised in the city of our God, in His holy mountain. Beautiful in elevation, the joy of the whole earth, is Mount Zion on the sides of the north, the city of the great King."

Psalm 48:1,2

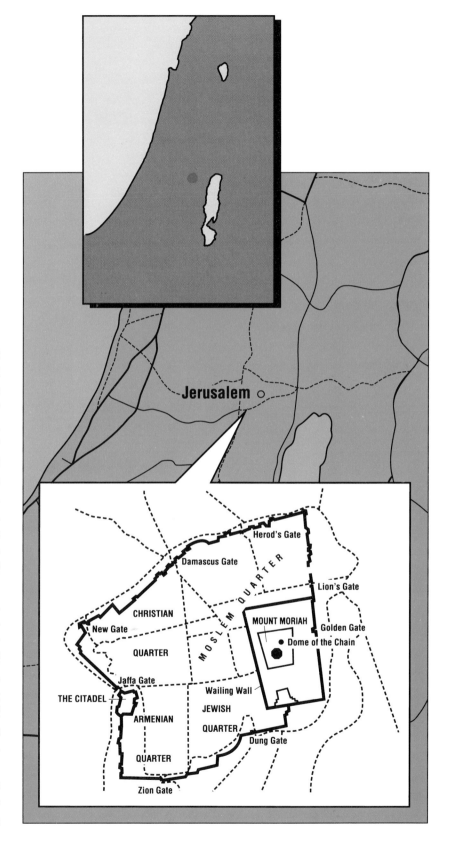

Have you ever walked through the streets of a city that just teemed with excitement? Perhaps you have paraded down the canyons of New York City or taken a leisurely stroll through the quaint cobblestone alleys of Paris. Or perhaps you wandered the streets of Athens with the glory that once belonged to Greece flashing before your eyes. Or possibly you find that the sidewalks of your hometown bring back precious memories of days gone by. But there is no city in the world that generates more excitement than the city of Jerusalem.

Sacred to the Jew, Muslim and Christian alike, Jerusalem has been the center of religious activity for thousands of years. The Jew venerates this city because it was the site of Solomon's Temple. The Muslim claims Jerusalem as the city from which the prophet Mohammed ascended into heaven. And, of course, Christians remember the city as the scene of the Lord's death, burial and resurrection.

Jerusalem alone can lay claim to being the "Holy City" (Isaiah 52:1; Nehemiah 11:1). Only Jerusalem is described as "the city which the

LORD had chosen out of all the tribes of Israel, to put His name there" (I Kings 14:21). The Bible identifies Jerusalem as the city of God (Psalm 48:1,2), the city of Jehovah (Isaiah 60:14), the mountain of the Lord (Isaiah 2:3) and the holy mountain (Isaiah 66:20). The Lord Himself refers to Jerusalem alone as "my city" (Isaiah 45:13) and frequently as "my holy mountain" (Isaiah 11:9). The first century A.D. Roman historian Pliny referred to Jerusalem as "by far the most famous city of the ancient Orient." Even today its importance cannot be overestimated.

The first appearance of the word "Jerusalem" in the Bible is in Joshua 10:1, but the city's prominence long predates that. The Tell el Amarna Tablets of the fifteenth century B.C. mention a city Urushalim. Genesis 14:18-20 records that the Patriarch Abraham paid tithes to "Melchizedek, king of Salem." Salem means peace. Jerusalem is the "city of peace." But no city in the world has been coveted and conquered more than Jerusalem. The Babylonians, Macedonians, Ptolemies, Seleucids, Romans, Byzantines, Persians, Arabs, Crusaders, Monguls, Mamelukes, Turks, British and Jordanians are only some of the conquerors of this great city.

To understand the layout of the present Old City, you must understand a number of things. This is a city accustomed to the hardship of war and the reorganization that subsequent periods of peace bring. The Walled City has existed as it is now for hundreds of years. In 1917, Great Britain issued the Balfour Declaration, which promised the Jews a national homeland in Palestine. This brought thousands of Jews back to Jerusalem. In 1948, however, when the British left Palestine, war broke out between the Jews and Arabs, and the Jews fled from the Old City to the western suburbs. A year later the Hashemite Kingdom of Jordan annexed the Walled City. The Jewish Quarter was razed, and 27 venerated and ancient synagogues were dismantled. For the next 20 years Jerusalem remained divided.

Then, suddenly, in 1967, Israeli forces moved

on the Old City during the Six Day War, and on June 28 the Old City was annexed by Israel. The wall separating Jewish West Jerusalem from Arab East Jerusalem came down. An era of urban expansion began, including restoration of the devastated Jewish Quarter. So today, as you enter the Walled City, held exclusively by the Arabs for so many years, you sense a decidedly Arab flavor but with the presence of Israeli soldiers and police. This is the new Old City.

JERUSALEM'S WALL

The shape of Jerusalem and the area covered by it has changed many times. Each change necessitated a wall encircling the city. Besieged and rebuilt, the Jerusalem wall has been totally destroyed at least five times. You may remember that the great lament of Nehemiah during Israel's captivity was that "the wall of Jerusalem is also broken down, and its gates are burned with fire" (Nehemiah 1:3).

The wall as it appears today is a conglomeration, and various periods of construction can be identified. Perhaps the oldest surviving section of the wall is Hasmonean, from the second century B.C. At the Citadel most of the visible wall dates from 1542 and was built by Sultan Suleiman "The Magnificent." In general, the lines of the present wall follow those of the wall scaled by the Crusaders in 1099, or they follow those that encompassed Hadrian's second-century Roman colony, Aelia Capitolina.

This uneven rectangular wall, which encloses the Ir Hakodesh (the Holy City), is the most striking feature of Jerusalem. Originally all Jerusalemites lived inside the wall. But in 1860, at the southwestern corner of the Old City, across the valley from Mount Zion, the first quarter outside the city wall was established. It is YEMIN MOSHE. One of Jerusalem's most distinctive Jewish landmarks is at its entrance, the MONTEFIORE WINDMILL. Although this may look like a little bit of "Holland in the Holy Land," the windmill was actually built by Sir Moses Montefiore as a flour mill, to provide the Jewish suburban settlers with work. Today only 5.45 percent of the city is housed within the wall.

The wall itself is massive, averaging 40 feet high. It is pierced by eight gates and punctuated with 34 towers. About two and one-half miles in length, the wall encompasses an area

of just over one-half mile square. If you are adventurous, you can walk along the top of this rampart wall and see Jerusalem in an exhilarating and distinctly unique manner. Although it is no longer possible to walk the entire circumference of the Old City on the wall, walking any part of it is an experience you'll treasure forever.

Above: The Cardo Maximus—Main street of Jerusalem in Roman times

Left: The Damascus Gate

JERUSALEM'S GATES

The stroll on top of the Jerusalem wall affords the opportunity to become acquainted with the positioning of the city's gates. Let's start at one of the most prominent gates and proceed clockwise around the city.

DAMASCUS GATE. It will be helpful if you superimpose the face of a clock over the Old City. At just about 12 o'clock the main gate of Old Jerusalem is positioned, the Damascus Gate. The road leading from Jerusalem to Damascus begins here. Because this road passes through Shechem, the gate is also called the Shechem Gate.

In Arabic, the gate has two other names. It

Above: **Herod's Gate**

Below: **The Eastern Gate**

Herod Antipas. However, it is more likely that Herod resided in the old Hasmonean Palace on Mount Zion. Nonetheless, Herod's name continues to be associated with this northern gate.

LION'S GATE. This prominent gate is at about two o'clock. It is so named because of the twin lions carved in relief on both sides of the entrance. These are the emblems of the Mameluke Sultan Baybars. The street passing through Lion's Gate leads to the Via Dolorosa. This gate is known to the Arabs as Saint Mary's Gate, because it leads to the Church of Mary's Tomb and the Kidron Valley.

The Lion's Gate has been known to Christians as Saint Stephen's Gate. It was believed that Stephen, the first Christian martyr, passed out of the city through this gate before he was stoned to death (Acts 7:54-60). However, the Church of Saint Stephen was built north of this point, at the gate now known as the Damascus Gate.

On June 7, 1967, the advancing Israeli armies penetrated the Lion's Gate and fought their way through the Old City to the Western (or Wailing) Wall. It was the first time in the city's long history that an invading force was successful in attacking Jerusalem from that direction.

GOLDEN GATE. This brings you due east to three o'clock and to the only one of

is called the "Gate of Victory," for it was long considered the only proper gate for royalty to enter. (It is somewhat more impressive than the other gates.) Also, it is known by local Arabs as the Gate of the Column. When Hadrian conquered the city, he celebrated that victory by building a victory column at the gate. The sixth-century Madeba map of Jerusalem (a mosaic map on a church floor in Jordan), shows a pillar just inside this gate. The pillar has long since disappeared.

In recent years archaeologists have been probing beneath the Damascus Gate. There you can see the northern gate of Hadrian's city, complete with a Roman inscription. Deep under the street that passes through the Damascus Gate is the Cardo Maximus, the main thoroughfare into the city during the era of the Roman Empire. It was intersected by the Decumanus, a street running into the city from the Jaffa Gate. These two streets effectively quartered ancient Jerusalem into what are today the Christian, Muslim, Jewish and Armenian Quarters.

HEROD'S GATE. At about one o'clock on your Jerusalem clock you will find Herod's Gate. You would expect a gate with a name like that to be an impressive entrance to a bustling quarter of the city. But it isn't. The gate apparently received its name from medieval pilgrims who believed the tradition that inside this gate was the residence of

Jerusalem's eight gates that is closed. It is commonly known as the "Golden Gate" but is sometimes called the "Eastern Gate." This is the oldest, the most celebrated and the most ornamental gate of the city; and it is the only one that leads directly to the Temple Mount. It is thought to have been built in the fifth century by Eudocia, wife of the Byzantine Emperor Theodosius II.

This double gate has twin arches. The northern arch is called the "Gate of Repentance," the southern arch, the "Gate of Mercy." It is believed that this was the site of the Closed Gate of the First Temple and the Shushan Gate of the Second Temple. It was clearly designed as the main entrance of both Old and New Testament Jerusalem. Jesus made His triumphal entry into Jerusalem through this gate (Matthew 21:8-11), and He left the city here to pray in the Garden of Gethsemane (Matthew 26:30,36).

The Kidron Valley below has long been associated with judgment, and it is said that the Turks blocked this gate in hopes of postponing the Day of Judgment. Others say it was closed to prevent the entry of the Messiah. Many Christians identify the Prince of Ezekiel 44:1-3 with Jesus Christ and believe that at our Lord's Second Coming the Golden Gate will be unblocked and He will enter the Temple Mount uninhibited.

Just outside this gate there is a Muslim cemetery that is overrun with dandelions and other wildflowers. It is officially off-limits to non-Muslims, but for a small "tip" the keeper of the cemetery will permit you to enter. Its entrance is at the Lion's Gate, and a short walk from there will bring you to the base of the Golden Gate, where you can get a fantastic photo of Jerusalem's premier gate.

DUNG GATE. Perhaps the least impressive of the eight gates, the Dung Gate is on the southern perimeter of the Jerusalem Wall at about six o'clock. It is sometimes known as the Gate of the Moors, for it leads to the Temple Mount through the inner Moors' Gate. In crusader times it was called the Tanner's Gate. But from the time of Nehemiah (Ne-

hemiah 2:13; 3:13,14; 12:31), it has been known as the Dung Gate. Jerusalemites for centuries have carted their garbage through this gate to the Hinnom Valley below.

ZION GATE. The gate at seven o'clock, which leads from the city to Mount Zion, is appropriately named "Zion Gate." The local Arab population prefers the name "Gate of David," for it gives access to the TOMB OF DAVID. Suleiman's wall slices Mount Zion in half and excludes the cenotaph marking the traditional site of David's tomb from his own city.

The Tomb of David, one of Judaism's holi-

Zion Gate

est shrines, is sacred also to Muslims and Christians. It is located in the same complex of buildings that houses the traditional Upper Room. Men must don a yarmulke (traditional little round Jewish hat) to enter. Inside a gloomy, miniscule room you will see a cenotaph covered with a thick cloth embroidered with a menorah over a star of David and with a border of lions standing on pillars. Above the cenotaph is an assortment of silver crowns and Torah scrolls.

As you round the southwestern corner of Jerusalem's Wall and turn north toward the Jaffa Gate, you pass one of Jerusalem's most prominent landmarks, the Tower of David.

JAFFA GATE. Located at nine o'clock, the Jaffa Gate is named "The Gate of the Friend" because of an Arabic inscription over the entrance which reads, "There is no god but Allah and Abraham is his friend."

The Jaffa Gate is one of Jerusalem's busiest. From here both the road to Bethlehem and Hebron and the road to Jaffa and the Mediterranean proceed. In preparation for the arrival of Kaiser Wilhelm II in 1898, the moat between the gate and the Citadel to the south was filled in, and the wall over the main entrance of the gate was breached to allow a mounted procession. In contrast, when General Allenby arrived at this gate, he dismounted his horse, as a mark of humility, before he entered the city.

NEW GATE. Walking north, with the Christian Quarter to your right, you arrive at the New Gate at about ten o'clock on the Jerusalem clock. It was built in 1887 by Sultan Abdul Hamid and was subsequently known as the "Gate of the Sultan."

Because Christian facilities outside the wall were expanding, the Sultan decided that a gate was needed to give ready access to the Christian Quarter. This gate was closed, along with the Zion and Jaffa Gates, during the Jordanian occupation of the city (1948-1967), because this side of Jerusalem faced territory held by the Israelis. Outside the gate is the Notre Dame de France and behind this the Russian Compound.

JERUSALEM'S CITADEL

One of two fortress-palaces built in Jerusalem by Herod the Great is to be found alongside the Jaffa Gate, forming its southern side. It is called THE CITADEL. (The other fortress is the Antonio, defense station for the Temple area.)

Herod's Citadel was constructed with three towers. The first was named after Phasael, Herod's brother; the second, after Hippicus, one of the king's close friends; and the third, after Mariamne, his Hasmonean wife whom he later murdered. So impressive were these towers that when Titus sacked Jerusalem in A.D. 70, he left the towers standing. But when Hadrian razed the city in A.D. 135, he destroyed most of the Citadel. Only Phasael's Tower and the fortress foundation survived. The Crusaders and Saracens rebuilt the Citadel much as you see it today, with five towers instead of the original three. Suleiman

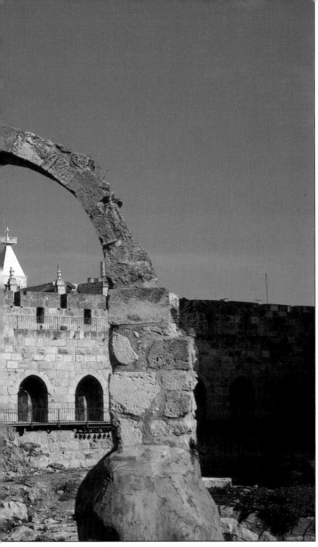

of the Christian Quarter, to your left, and of the Armenian Quarter, to your right.

Now descend to the courtyard. You will see the remains of the ancient Hasmonean wall slicing across the courtyard. From here you can also distinguish the five towers of the Citadel. You have just come from the northeast tower, Phasael's Tower. The northwest tower is actually the southern tower of the Jaffa Gate. The southwest tower sits on Crusader stones with Mameluke and Turkish restorations on top of them. The southeast tower is entirely Mameluke. Perhaps the most recognizable tower is the southern tower. This is the Minaret Tower, which can be seen for miles. The minaret was not added until 1665.

If you visit the Citadel between April and October, you are in for a special treat. Each evening, except for Fridays and holidays, a SOUND AND LIGHT PERFORMANCE is presented within the Citadel's precincts. At different times you can hear the performance in Hebrew, French or English. It is entitled "A Stone in David's Tower" and tells the story of 4000 years of history at this site. It is excellent.

completed the project in 1540.

All except the western side of the fortress, the Jerusalem wall side, is surrounded by a moat. Only part of the moat is visible today. Access to the Citadel is gained through an eastern gate inside the city. Go up the stairs and through an arch; then cross the moat over a small bridge and arrive at the main gate. Inside the gate and straight ahead you can see an interesting second-century Roman sarcophagus that is highly decorated. The stairway to the right leads to Phasael's Tower. (This is also known as "David's Tower" because of the mistaken belief that this was the original site of the City of David.)

The large rough-cut stones which comprise the lower 60 feet of the tower are clearly Herodian. They are identical to those of the Western Wall or the lower portion of the Pinnacle of the Temple. From the top of the tower you get a good view of the Old City, especially

David's Tower

JERUSALEM'S QUARTERS

During the rule of the ancient Roman Empire, Jerusalem was divided into quarters by two intersecting streets. From the Damascus Gate, the Cardo Maximus split the city into east and west. From the Jaffa Gate, the Decumanus sliced the city into north and south. Roughly, these four quarters still exist in the twentieth century. Here are the most important sites for a Christian to visit in each.

THE CHRISTIAN QUARTER. If you enter the Old City at the Jaffa Gate and proceed down David Street, the Christian Quarter lies entirely to your left. This quarter is filled with churches, hospices, chapels, monasteries, schools and missions. The best shopping in this quarter is along this street and the tiny adjoining alleys.

The major street leading from David Street into this sector is Christian Quarter Road. It's your first left. Off this road and up the terraced street called Khan el Khubat, is HEZEKIAH'S POOL, 2000 years old. Now surrounded by buildings and no longer used, the 250-foot-long, 148-foot-wide pool has a bed ten feet below street level. It is identified by Josephus as the Pool of Amygdalon ("Almond Pool" in Greek or "Great Tower" in Hebrew).

The actual Pool of Hezekiah is probably located elsewhere.

Off Christian Quarter Road, on the other side, is the MURISTAN, a Greek Bazaar. In Arabic, Muristan means "hospice," and during Crusader times it served as such. During the second century this area was the Forum of Jerusalem. In 1869, the Turks divided this area between the Greek Orthodox, who built this arcade and the ornamental MURISTAN FOUNTAIN at its entrance, and the Lutherans, who built the Church of the Redeemer at the arcade entrance. In the bazaar you can see an assortment of leather luggage, sheepskins, baskets, and more.

THE CHURCH OF THE REDEEMER was built over the gateway to the cloisters of the Crusader Church of Saint Mary Latina in 1898. It includes some of the architectural relics of the twelfth-century church. The present church's northern portal is the preserved gateway to the Crusader Church.

The real reason to stop here is the view from the tower of the church. It is near the center of the walled city, and the tower provides a magnificent platform from which to take pictures of Jerusalem.

From this vantage point you can get a pho-

An Arab potter

to of the temple area, from the west, just as perfect as the photo you can take of Jerusalem from in front of the Seven Arches Hotel, on the Mount of Olives, from the east.

North of the Muristan is the most important church of the city, the Church of the Holy Sepulchre, held by many to be the site of Jesus' crucifixion. (It will be discussed in detail in the next chapter.) South of the Muristan, toward David Street, is the CHURCH OF SAINT JOHN THE BAPTIST, believed to be the oldest church in Jerusalem. The present church dates from the eleventh century and incorporates the remains of several ancient churches. Excavations under this building have revealed a crypt dating from the fifth century or earlier. In this crypt was a reliquary which purportedly contained a piece of Christ's cross.

THE MUSLIM QUARTER. At the north and northeast sector of the city is the Mus-

lim (Moslem) Quarter. Here you will find the finest examples of Mameluke architecture in the city. Here, too, is the Old City's most famous street, the Via Dolorosa. Several other sites are of interest as well.

Starting from the Lion's Gate, enter the Muslim Quarter on Saint Mary's Street. The first building on your right is the Greek Orthodox Church of Saints Joachim and Anna. Just a few feet farther is the entry door to one of Jerusalem's oldest and most beautiful churches—the CHURCH OF SAINT ANNE. Designed in the Burgundian Romanesque style, this is one of the finest examples of Crusader construction in the Holy Land. Enter through the Gothic doorway at the back of the church and look first at the ceiling. Notice that the pointed arches divide the church into thirds. The vaulted ceiling and beautiful dome make this a spectacular structure.

This church was constructed in 1140 by Yvette, daughter of Balwin II, king of Jerusalem. The Saracens converted it to a Muslim seminary. Napoleon III restored the building and in 1878 committed it to the care of the White Fathers, a Greek Orthodox missionary order whose members wear white habits.

Left: The Church of the Holy Sepulchre

Below: Flowers at the Church of Saint Anne

In the right nave of the church, about half-way to the altar, there is a set of stairs that leads to a crypt under the church. A fourth-century tradition states that in this crypt the virgin Mary was born of Joachim and Anne. Hence, the church is named in honor of Mary's mother.

Go back outside to the beautiful garden. Prior to 1956 there were a number of old buildings to the right. When they were demolished, the White Fathers began to excavate the site. Here they discovered the POOL OF BETHESDA. According to the Gospel of John, "There is in Jerusalem by the Sheep Gate a pool, which is called in Hebrew, Bethesda, having five porches" (John 5:2). Here Jesus performed a great miracle. A man impotent for 38 years lay by the pool, awaiting opportunity to get into the water and be healed. "Jesus said to him, 'Rise, take up your bed and walk'" (John 5:8). And he did.

Right: **The Via Dolorosa**

Below: **The Pool of Bethesda**

Excavations have revealed a fifth-century church at the site, the Church of the Paralytic. It was destroyed by the Persians in 614. However, the Crusaders built a chapel over

the remains. The apse and entrance of this chapel are still visible at the southern end of the pool. The water level at the pool is nearly 60 feet below the current ground level, but for the surefooted, the climb down to the "house of mercy" (which is what Bethesda means) is possible.

This quarter has the best shopping in all of Jerusalem. Continue into the city on the Via Dolorosa, and when it turns sharply left, bear sharply right on El-Wad Road. This leads you directly to the Damascus Gate and a bonanza of things to buy. If you enter the quarter through the Damascus Gate and descend the platform steps, go to the right on Suq Khan Ez-Zeit.

Here the street narrows quickly. Men sit around smoking water pipes and playing shaish-baish, a sort of backgammon. The street is occasionally blocked by an overloaded donkey. You can't help but smell the spices, the Turkish coffee, the donkey. Here you can buy Arab pastries, fruit and vegetables, mother-of-pearl items, olive-wood

carvings, brass trinkets, silver necklaces, sheepskin jackets—and just about anything else. Raw quarters of lamb, goat and beef hang at the front of the meat markets. You may be tempted to shoo away the flies.

In this delightful bazaar, you can barter and bargain until you're convinced you have the "steal" of the century. But the glint in the Arab shopkeeper's eye might cause you to think otherwise. If you don't see what you want in this shop, go across the street to where the shopkeeper's "brother" has "a good deal for you." Enjoy this Muslim Quarter. It's like nothing you've ever seen before.

THE JEWISH QUARTER. The Jewish Quarter is immediately west of the Western Wall and the Dung Gate, on the eastern flank of Mount Zion, overlooking the Temple Mount. This was the first suburb Jerusalem ever had. David established his city on the Ophel, the area on the slopes south of the Temple Mount. When the population filled that site, the overflow settled here. Archaeological excavations show Jewish settlements here dating to the seventh and eighth centuries B.C. This became the Upper City, in

distinction from the original Lower City.

During the days of Herod this Upper City flourished, and elegant Greek-style homes of the very wealthy were built here. This quarter, however, was destroyed by Titus when the city was sacked in A.D. 70. Both Rome and Byzantium barred the Jews from returning to this site. It was not until the noted biblical commentator Rabbi Moshe ben-Nachman, the Ramban, arrived in Jerusalem in 1267 that a synagogue was established here. This sector of the city then became the center of Jewish life in the Holy City for nearly 700 years.

In the 1948 War of Independence, the Arab Legion drove the Jews out of this quarter and began to destroy their synagogues systematically. When the Israeli forces reunited Jerusalem in 1967, the Jews began to clear the rubble and restore it.

Today in the Jewish Quarter, you see ongoing restoration.

From the end of David Street, where it becomes Chain Street, turn right on Jewish Quarter Street to RAMBAN SYNAGOGUE. You can also reach it from the Dung Gate or the Lion's Gate. Ramban, the oldest synagogue in the Old City, was named in honor of Rabbi Moshe ben-Nachman. Jews worshipped in this synagogue until 1585, when the Mufti of Jerusalem turned it into a mosque. Immediately after entering this decrepit synagogue in 1967, Israeli soldiers had it reconsecrated.

Outside of the synagogue is a minaret, the only one in the Jewish Quarter. South of it is the YOHANAN BEN ZAKKAI SYNAGOGUE, which is sometimes called the "Four Synagogues," because it consists of four interconnected rooms. It was built in 1586 to compensate for the loss of the Ramban the year before, and it has been the spiritual center for the Sephardic (Spanish) Jews for centuries. The synagogue was given the name because tradition indicates that this was the site of the distinguished rabbi's school. According to an ancient legend, Ben Zakkai's Synagogue had a secret tunnel that led directly to the temple, but no evidence of a tunnel ever existed.

The Old City

amidst all her utensils. This stop in the Jewish Quarter will take you back to that fateful day when God's city was completely and suddenly destroyed.

Nearby is the WOHL ARCHAEOLOGICAL MUSEUM, which is actually a subterranean look at a Herodian mansion. This massive excavation reveals how a family of moderate means would have lived in the time of Jesus. You will see rooms with beautiful mosaic floors, tables, juglets, amphoras and other everyday artifacts of the first century A.D. Of special interest is the burnt section which, like the Burnt House, gives evidence of the destruction of this lovely home. It's a trip back in time—and a very interesting one.

THE ARMENIAN QUARTER. The Armenian Quarter is located in the southwestern sector of Old Jerusalem, on the northern slope of Mount Zion. You can reach it through the Zion Gate or the Jaffa Gate. This quarter is almost a city within a city.

The Armenian Compound contains a museum, library, seminary, monastery, schools—and more. If you turn onto Saint James Street, off Armenian Patriarchate Street, then turn left on Ararat, you arrive at SAINT MARK'S HOUSE. This is the Syrian Orthodox Monastery and the See of the Syrian Archbishop of Jerusalem. The building, which dates from the twelfth century, is very important to the Armenian Church. The Armenians believe that this is the house of Mary, Mark's mother, where Peter went after being delivered from prison (Acts 12:12). Here, they say, Peter founded the first church. Also, they believe that the Upper Room was here.

After you return to Armenian Patriarchate Road and walk a short distance south, you soon come to one of Jerusalem's most gorgeous cathedrals, SAINT JAMES CATHEDRAL. Two saints named James are associated with this Crusader structure. James the fisherman, the brother of John, was beheaded by Herod Agrippa, grandson of Herod the Great, in A.D. 44 (Acts 12:1,2). The other James is James the Less, another of the Lord's disciples.

The ornate cathedral is richly carpeted with

When excavations of the Upper City of Jerusalem began in 1970, the first layers of debris cleared away were all modern. Then, suddenly, the archaeologists came upon a house that had been destroyed by fire. It was determined that the house, dubbed THE BURNT HOUSE, caught fire when the Roman soldiers attacked Jerusalem in A.D. 70. Everything in the house was instantly engulfed in flames. When the roof caved in, the house was sealed for exactly 1900 years. In the kitchen of the Burnt House was a young woman who sank to the floor near the doorway when the house collapsed. Her skeleton was found thick oriental rugs. Hanging from the ceiling are alternating lamps of gold and silver with porcelain ostrich eggs as ornamentation. On the walls and pillars are antique blue and green tiles of glazed earthenware. Around the walls hang dark canvases that are reproductions of the pictures of Armenian saints and kings painted on the walls. Adjacent to the altar is the very ornate, onion-domed throne of Saint James (the Less). The Armenians believe he is the James who was the first Christian bishop of Jerusalem. Most Christians identify James, the brother of our Lord, as the head of the early church in Jerusalem (Acts 12:17; 15:13; 21:18; Galatians 1:19). James the Less is reputedly buried under the great altar of the church.

As you leave the church, be sure to look to your right. Here is a chapel decorated with tortoise-shell and silver gates, which is claimed by the Armenian clergy to be the spot where James the Greater was beheaded by Herod.

One final site is worth your attention. Near the Zion Gate at the extreme southern end of the Armenian Quarter is the HOUSE OF ANNAS. According to John 18:13, before He was led to the Sanhedrin for judgment, Jesus was escorted to the house of Annas, the father-in-law of Caiaphas, the High Priest. You enter the fifth-century church at the site through a portico. Beautifully decorated, as all Armenian churches are, the House of Annas is adorned with gilded carvings, tiled walls, old paintings and an altar similar to that of the Saint James Cathedral.

Once you leave the Armenian Quarter, you leave behind a world unto itself. Aramaic is commonly spoken in the Armenian Quarter. You may have heard priests, bishops or archbishops pray in a strange language. That was Aramaic. This segment of Christianity has followed its own language, customs, calendar and beliefs since they separated from the mainstream of Christianity in A.D. 491.

JERUSALEM'S WESTERN WALL

When you return to the Dung Gate, you will find the most direct entrance to Jerusalem's

A ROMAN DINNER

For a very entertaining and delightful evening, visit THE CARDO CULINARIA for dinner. Located at about the middle of the CARDO, the ancient Roman main street that bisected Jerusalem in the Roman period, the Cardo Culinaria was established in the late 1980's to acquaint modern travelers with Roman meals and customs. Your dinner at the Culinaria will feature only Roman dinnerware (no fork), a triclinium table (a U-shaped, three-couch arrangement from the first century) and delicious recipes from the Roman Cookery of Apicius (a gourmet chef of Imperial Rome). Dressed in your own toga, you'll enjoy a full evening of entertainment—including flutists, harpists and jugglers.

most famous wall, the WESTERN WALL. It was formerly called the Wailing Wall, but its designation changed after the Six Day War of 1967. Legend has it that early in the morning heavy drops of dew form on the wall and run down like tears. Local citizens say it is the

Jews praying at the Wall

wall's way of weeping with Israel in her exile. Actually, it was called the Wailing Wall because for centuries Jews would flock to the wall to bemoan their loss. The Ninth of Av, the anniversary of the Temple's destruction, was a special day of mourning.

When the Jews were driven out of Jerusalem by the Arab Legion in 1948, they were unable to assemble at the wall as usual. For 20 years they had waited impatiently. When the opportunity presented itself during the Six Day War of 1967, Israeli soldiers cut a path right through the Old City to the wall. On June 7, 1967, General Moshe Dayan said, "We have returned to our holy places, never to part from them again." It was this place he had in mind. Now the Wailing Wall is known simply as the Western Wall. It has become a scene of joy, a celebration of prayer and singing; occasionally people dance spontaneously. Israeli bulldozers have cleared a large esplanade before the wall to accommodate tens of thousands of worshippers and visitors.

As you pass through the Dung Gate and go up the slight grade to the esplanade, you will notice the archaeological excavations to your right, in the area south of the Temple Mount. Digging began there in 1968 but was stopped by the ultra-orthodox Jews of the Mea Shearim

Right: **Jerusalem's Western Wall**

Below: **Excavations west of the temple wall**

district who believe this area was once a cemetery and that the modern archaeologists are therefore in violation of Jewish desecration laws. The excavations, however, yielded a wealth of information about Jerusalem in Jesus' day. Especially interesting are the steps leading to the DOUBLE GATE of the Temple and the steps leading to the TRIPLE GATE. A council house and a ritual bathhouse were also discovered.

Ahead you will find a checkpoint. Because this wall is extremely sacred to the Jews, everyone must pass through a security check and open their handbags, camera cases and so forth.

At the wall, men and women are separated by a fence. Women must be modestly dressed; men must don a yarmulke. (One is provided as you approach the wall.) Torah scrolls are found at spaced intervals along the wall. Hasidim Jews, with their phylacteries and prayer books, bob and weave as they chant their rituals.

Notice the sprigs of grass growing out of the cracks in the upper level of the wall. Now look at the cracks at eye level. Tiny strips of paper have been rolled up and slipped into the cracks. These are prayers that visitors to the site have placed there in hope that Jehovah would look kindly on them.

Make your way through the group of praying orthodox Jews—young and old—to the northern side of the wall. (Unfortunately,

THE SACRED WALL OF THE JEWS

Why is this wall so sacred to the Jews?

The Temple of Solomon was situated on an enlarged Mount Moriah. The expanded area was buttressed by retaining walls. When Herod rebuilt the temple, he extended these walls even farther. Much of the retaining wall stands today.

Many Christians mistakenly identify the Western Wall with that of Solomon's Temple; it is not. In fact, it isn't even the wall of the Second Temple, but it is part of the retaining wall of that temple. Nevertheless, of the Herodian walls that survived the destruction of Jerusalem in A.D. 70, this Western Wall is closest to the original temple sanctuary. Thus, it is held as the most sacred Jewish site in the Holy Land.

The wall is 60 feet high and 91 feet long. Each stone is finely cut and beveled, and no mortar was ever used in the wall. The oblong stones of Herod's wall are capped by four tiers of smooth Roman blocks and about a dozen tiers of smaller stones from a Turkish wall. You can distinguish them easily.

The wall is impressive. Even more impressive is the fact that 60 feet of the wall is underground. Fourteen more courses of huge Herodian stones are beneath you. When Titus razed the temple, he ordered the rubble to be cast over the wall into the Tyropoeon Valley, between the Upper City and the Temple Mount. If you look down WARREN'S SHAFT (an excavation hole), you'll be able to see down to the base of the wall.

women cannot follow, as this section is accessible only through the men's side of the esplanade.) You will pass under an arch that at one time spanned the Tyropoeon Valley. It is named WILSON'S ARCH after the British officer who explored it in 1850.

It's almost impossible to conceive that the flat area in front of the Western Wall was once 60 feet lower, in a valley leading from the center of Jerusalem to the Hinnom Valley on the south. But to imagine that two great arches once spanned this valley is even more incredible.

If you return to the base of the ramp leading to the wall at the Moors' Gate, you will be able to see a small ledge of a second arch. This is ROBINSON'S ARCH, named for the American scholar Edward Robinson (1836). This tiny bit of stone was once part of a mighty bridge used to provide passage from the tem-

Above: **The esplanade at the Western Wall**

Below: **Jewish man praying**

ple site to the upper city, home of royalty.

Your final glimpse of the Western Wall comes as you proceed up the ramp toward the top of the wall. This entrance to the Temple Mount is the MOORS' GATE. Here again you will encounter an Israeli soldier who will ask to inspect handbags and other things you are carrying. After a brief delay you will enter the Temple Mount itself. What a thrill! You are standing on one of the most sacred parcels of real estate in the world. No spot on earth has been more sought after or more fought over than the 35 acres within the walls of the Temple Compound.

JERUSALEM'S TEMPLE AREA

The sites you will visit in this area are Muslim sites of the holy area which they call HAREM ESH SHARIF. As you proceed from the Moors' Gate, you will come to the EL AKSA MOSQUE, ahead on your right. As you approach the entrance, you may notice to your left a small sunken fountain. It is circular, with a single row of pinkish marble seats at its base, each equipped with a faucet from the fountain. Known as EL KAS, The Cup, this fountain is used by the Muslims as an ablution pool, a place to ritually wash before entering the holy places. All Muslims must

do this before entering El Aksa. As a visitor, you must remove your shoes, leaving them outside. Whatever you carry will be searched before you enter each of the shrines on the Temple Mount. In 1969, an insane Australian tourist set fire to El Aksa, and now precautions are taken to prevent further desecration of the shrines.

El Aksa, which means the "distant place" (from Mecca), is Islam's third holiest shrine, after Mecca and Medina. It was erected on the foundation of a Byzantine church and still follows the general lines of a basilica. It was constructed between 709 and 715, and its architect was Caliph al Waleed, son of Abd el Malik. It has been destroyed and rebuilt on numerous occasions. The Crusaders captured it in 1099 and El Aksa became the headquarters for the Knights Templars. But in 1187 Saladin returned the building to the Muslims.

You enter the shrine through the seven (pointed) arches of the facade that faces the Dome of the Rock. The floors are covered with lush, priceless oriental rugs which present your feet with cushiony and welcome relief from the stones of Jerusalem. In 1951, the Jordanian King Abdullah was assassinated here. His grandson, now King Hussein, was at his side. A stray bullet scarred the pillar just inside the door to your left.

This mosque is 5260 square yards, built in basilica fashion with a large central nave bounded by triple aisles on either side. Assemblies of about 5000 worshippers are possible. A row of 21 windows made from stained glass from Hebron is on both sides of the nave, high on the walls. The lead dome at the far end of the mosque is supported by arched columns. The gleaming whiteness of the marble pillars throughout the mosque actually makes the place quite cheery in comparison to other Muslim shrines. The chandeliers hanging from the ceiling are gorgeous.

To the right, as you leave the mosque, there is an enclosure containing a 16-step stairway leading to ANCIENT AKSA, a little-used mosque below El Aksa. It is much older and at least as interesting as the mosque you've just left but is usually not open to the public.

A bit farther to the east, toward the Mount of Olives, there is a strange-looking, sealed stone structure. It is known as THE GREAT SEA and is the cap to one of many cisterns under the paved surface of the Haram, the temple area. The estimated capacity of these underground cisterns is ten million gallons. The 40-foot-deep Great Sea itself has a capacity of two million gallons.

These cisterns are not the only subterranean structures at the Temple Mount. If you were permitted to walk toward the extreme southeast corner of the Temple area, you would walk directly over SOLOMON'S STABLES. Not generally open to the public, the little building with the iron gate at the southeast corner gives access to a broad staircase that descends into cavernous stables.

These are actually the work of Herod the Great, not Solomon. When the prolific builder expanded the temple area, he built up this corner with a platform supported by a series of 88 pillared arches. All of this was done 170 feet above the floor of the Kidron Valley. The external wall on the south plainly displays the blocked arches of the Triple Gate of the Second Temple. Evidently Herod used the area under the vaulted platform for stabling horses, as did the Crusaders centuries later.

It used to be possible to take a short walk along the eastern wall to a narrow stone stairway that leads right to the top of the wall, to the PINNACLE OF THE TEMPLE. However, for years the security police have not permitted tourists to go there.

The second of the three temptations of Christ occurred here. "Then the devil took Him up into the holy city, set Him on a pinnacle of the temple" (Matthew 4:5). The Devil told Jesus that if He was truly the Son of God, He could cast Himself off the pinnacle and the angels would bear Him up in their hands (Psalm 91:11,12).

Return to the center of the Temple Mount.

THE SIGNIFICANCE OF MOUNT MORIAH

MOUNT MORIAH is a rocky knoll of Judea that is much like any one of a thousand others in the Holy Land, except that it is much more significant. Abraham was commanded by God to take his only son Isaac to Mount Moriah and sacrifice him to Jehovah (Genesis 22:1-14). This knoll contained the threshingfloor of Araunah, which was purchased by King David. Here he built an altar and offered burnt offerings and peace offerings to God, staying a great plague in Israel (II Samuel 24:15-25). On this knoll, David gathered the materials for the magnificent Temple of God, which his son Solomon built (I Chronicles 21:18—22:5; II Chronicles 3:1-7,11). The treasures of the house of God were taken from Mount Moriah when the temple was destroyed by Nebuchadnezzar in 587 B.C., at the time of the Babylonian captivity. When the exiles returned, Nehemiah and the people built a wall around this rocky knoll (Nehemiah 2:4-20; 6:15,16). Here Herod the Great rebuilt the temple.

After the Roman general Titus destroyed Herod's Temple and the city of Jerusalem, the Roman Emperor Hadrian paganized this holy mount by erecting a temple to Jupiter. In fact, in A.D. 138 Hadrian rebuilt the city, naming it Aelia Capitolina; and he forbade the Jews from entering the city on penalty of death. In 639, Jerusalem fell into the hands of the Muslims, and Mount Moriah became a Muslim shrine.

Beyond El Kas is a raised platform that may be ascended by any one of eight staircases. Over each staircase is an arcade. Muslim legend says that scales that weigh the souls of men at the Great Judgment Day will be hung from these arcades. You may mount the platform by ascending the broad staircase from the south. The graceful structure immediately to your left is the SUMMER PULPIT, erected in 1456 by Burhan ed Din. It resembles the pulpits in European cathedrals.

Looking at the
Dome of the Rock
through the
southern arches

Straight ahead is the most prominent feature of this temple area. In fact, it is the most recognizable edifice in the Holy Land—the DOME OF THE ROCK.

When Caliph Omar captured Jerusalem in 637, he cleared the site of rubble and built a wooden mosque where the temple once stood. Because of this, many pilgrims mistakenly refer to the Dome of the Rock as the Mosque of Omar. Actually, there is a Mosque of Omar in Jerusalem, just opposite the entrance to the Church of the Holy Sepulchre. The Dome of the Rock was built by Caliph Abd el Malik in 685-705.

The mosque is octagonal in design and has a huge golden dome. The base is 180 feet high with a diameter of 78 feet. The upper half of its exterior is decorated mainly with blue tiles, although green, yellow and white tiles are also visible. The lower half is white stone. The cylinder on the roof, on which the golden dome sits, is covered with tiles in patterns that resemble bead work of the American Indians. The dome itself is an aluminum brass alloy from Italy. There are four entrances to the mosque, each under a rounded roof that is supported by pillars. The entrance gates are the Mecca Gate on the south, the Gate of the Judgment of David on the east, the Gate of Paradise on the north and the Western Gate. To enter, you must take off your shoes.

Inside, you are treated to the sight of stained-glass windows, intricate mosaics of grapes, date palms, fruit, corn and painted and gilded arabesques in colors of red, black and gold reflecting from the dome. No design is ever repeated. Since Greek architects were employed in the mosque's design, the interior has a definite Byzantine flavor. The carpets are colorful. The golden frieze at the base of the dome is inscribed with verses from the Koran. But the central attraction under the dome is the summit of Mount Moriah, which protrudes through the floor of the mosque some seven feet. This immense rough-hewn rock measures approximately 40 x 50 feet. However, a wooden wall surrounds it, and you can see the rock only on tiptoe or at the one opening at the southeast corner.

Once thought to be the center of the world (and depicted as such on maps), this rock is the focal point of both the Israelite and Islamic religions. The Holy of Holies may have been here. For Islam, the site is sacred because tradition says that it was from the surface of this massive rock that Mohammed ascended into heaven.

As you make your way around to the opening in the wooden wall, you will see a flight of stairs descending through an arched marble doorway. The steps lead down to a cave beneath the rock known to the Muslims as the "Well of Souls" but generally referred to as the GROTTO OF THE SACRED ROCK. Legend says that twice a week the dead meet here to pray. Once you are in the cave under the rock, you can see a hole in the ceiling said to be the drain which carried the blood from the altar of the Jewish Temple.

Once you make your way around the rock, you can file out through the tiny foyer at the western entrance. A local joke is that, since so many pairs of shoes are lined up outside, you now have a chance to pick out the best pair possible. Proceed around the Dome of the Rock to the eastern side and to the DOME OF THE CHAIN. This eighth-century miniature Dome of the Rock is tiled like the original and was built by Abd el Malik as well. It was used by the Arabs as a treasury for storing silver. The Crusaders used it as a church, calling it the Chapel of Saint James.

This little dome exhibits an interesting phenomenon. It is constructed with 6 inner and 11 outer pillars, and no matter where you stand you can see all 17 pillars at the same time.

Leave the raised platform through the eastern arcade and go down the steps. Head across the grassy area to the Golden Gate. The lit-

tle path to the right leads to the interior of this seventh-century gate, which looks somewhat like a square building with two arches in the back. You can climb to the top of the gate for a breathtaking view of the Kidron Valley. No wonder this is where Solomon built his opulent temple. It had a magnificent view. But what would you expect? This is Jerusalem, the city of God.

The Dome of the Rock

CHAPTER TWELVE

ETERNAL PLACES

FOLLOWING JESUS' FINAL STEPS

*"So they took Jesus and led Him away. And He, bearing His cross,
went out to a place called the Place of a Skull, which is called
in Hebrew, Golgotha, where they crucified Him."*

John 19:16-18

The date was July 20, 1969. The time, 4:17.45 Eastern Daylight Time. The place, 240,000 miles from Jerusalem. The event—the Eagle had landed. For the first time in history man had reached an "unearthly" body. Neal Armstrong stepped outside the spacecraft and said, "That's one small step for man, one giant leap for mankind." Do you remember where you were on that historic occasion?

In the excitement of the hour the president of the United States proclaimed that this was the "greatest day of our lives." Most Christians, born again by the grace of God, would have to respectfully disagree with the president. For the Christian, many days supersede this one in eternal importance, especially the days when Jesus walked on this earth. As you follow His final footsteps, you will visit places associated with those days.

The events of Christ's final week are chronologically disputed. But if we follow the

Palm Sunday Street

traditional timetable, these events look something like this.

SUNDAY, A.M. Having spent a quiet weekend in Bethany with friends (Matthew 26:6-13; John 11:55—12:11), Jesus sent two of His disciples to BETHPHAGE to get a colt (Luke 19:28-30). There, in a tiny hamlet on the eastern slopes of the Mount of Olives, the final week began. In fact, when you visit a Franciscan convent there, you can see the STELE OF BETHPHAGE, a stone which tradition claims to be the very stone from which Jesus mounted the colt. Paintings on the cubical rock date back to the time of the Crusaders.

The tiny path over the Mount of Olives leads past the Pater Noster Church to the Kidron Valley and the Golden Gate of Jerusalem's Eastern Wall. (It's possible that a bridge spanned the Kidron in Jesus' day.) This was the route of our Lord's Triumphal Entry into Jerusalem. Palm branches were placed in His path. Crowds shouted, "Hosanna! Blessed is He who comes in the name of the Lord!" (John 12:13). When the Pharisees called on Jesus to repudiate this unsolicited adoration, the Master replied, "I tell you that if these should keep silent, the stones would immediately cry out" (Luke 19:40).

SUNDAY, P.M. When the Messiah entered the temple, the chant "Hosanna to the son of David" continued, angering the chief priests and scribes (Matthew 21:15). At this point, Jesus cleansed the temple for the second time, overturning the money-changers' tables and exhorting, "My house shall be called a house of prayer, but you have made it a den of thieves" (Matthew 21:13).

At day's end Jesus returned to Bethany.

MONDAY, A.M. Early in the morning Jesus and His disciples made the return trip to Jerusalem. While skirting the Mount of Olives, they passed a fig tree. Jesus examined it and found it leafy but fruitless. This was unusual, for a fig tree bears over a ten-month period and the fruit precedes the flower. Jesus cursed the tree and used the occasion to teach His disciples (Matthew 21:19; Mark 11:14). The judgment of the tree symbolized the coming judgment on the ritual emptiness of the temple worship. Apparently, He returned to Bethany again for the night.

TUESDAY, A.M. This day found the Lord Jesus teaching in the outer court of the temple. Here He was approached by the chief priests and the elders, who were obviously disturbed by the events of the last two days. Their questions, "By what authority are You doing these things?" and "Who gave you this authority?" (Matthew 21:23), show their continued spiritual blindness to the messianic claims of Jesus. Their challenge gave occasion for three parables (Matthew 21:28—22:14).

The Lord was next assailed by the Pharisees and Herodians. Their crafty question about tribute to Caesar brought Jesus' classic response, "Render therefore to Caesar the things that are Caesar's, and to God the things that are God's" (Matthew 22:21).

Then it was the Sadducees' turn, and they asked a question about the resurrection. After astonishing them with His answer, Jesus turned and spoke to the multitude at large. The pronouncement of woes upon the scribes and Pharisees and the characterization of them as hypocrites, blind guides and whited sepulchers was the last straw. Violent confrontation was inevitable.

Jerusalem figs

TUESDAY, NOON. Jesus left the temple and walked through the Kidron Valley to the Mount of Olives. During the afternoon, He delivered His Olivet discourse, the sermon on the coming Tribulation.

TUESDAY, P.M. The battle lines began to form. Jesus returned to Bethany, to the house of Simon the leper. The chief priests, scribes and elders assembled themselves in secret sessions at the house of Caiaphas, and they "plotted to take Jesus by trickery and kill Him" (Matthew 26:4). Judas stole away from the Bethany assembly and went to the Sanhedrin. His offer to betray Jesus in the privacy of Gethsemane's Garden, away from His numerous supporters, was met with quick approval.

That night Jesus slept, the disciples slept, the Sanhedrin slept. But Judas—how could he sleep?

WEDNESDAY. A day of silence. Perhaps for the weary Master and His disciples it was a day of rest and reflection at their retreat in Bethany.

THURSDAY, A.M. Rest continues. The events of this day seem to have begun in the afternoon.

THURSDAY, NOON. Jesus dispatched Peter and John to Jerusalem to prepare for the Passover. They were told to follow a man carrying a water pitcher to "a large upper room, furnished and prepared" (Mark 14:12-15). In Jewish and Arab homes, carrying water was the task of the women. This man would easily be identified.

THURSDAY, P.M. By evening, Jesus and His disciples had entered Jerusalem and made their way to the UPPER ROOM. The traditional site of this room is on Mount Zion in the complex of buildings just below the CHURCH OF THE DORMITION (also known as the Dormition Abbey). Near the Zion Gate, the abbey stands at the supposed site of Mary's death. The Upper Room and the Tomb of David occupy the same complex of buildings nearby.

From the parking lot below the abbey, take the path that leads to the vaulted first floor of the triple-domed complex. Go through the stone arch and take a sharp left up a narrow outside stairway. Some years ago these stone steps, which featured deep indentations caused by repeated footsteps, had to be re-treaded for safety. At the top, turn left through a hallway with paneless windows. Go across a narrow terrace and into the traditional Upper Room.

The architectural craftsmanship is that of the Crusaders. The massive room features a rib-vaulted ceiling supported by tree-like columns. Known as the Coenaculum or CENACLE (meaning "dining hall"), this room is one of two surviving from the Byzantine Church of Saint Mary on Mount Zion. This building was sacked but was later rebuilt in 1335 by the Franciscans. In 1551, this order was expelled; and the complex fell into the hands of the Muslims, who consecrated it as a mosque to the Prophet David. In 1948, it was returned to Israeli hands.

Jesus instituted the Lord's Supper at this site (Matthew 26:17-30; Luke 22:7-30). Also, the apostles reportedly met here to regroup after Christ's ascension into heaven (Acts 1:13,14). Some believe that the 120 disciples were assembled in this upper room when the Holy Ghost came upon them on the Day of Pentecost (Acts 2:1-42). These events make this site one of the most important in Christendom.

After the supper was over, Jesus and the Eleven—Judas having departed—walked through the moonlit streets of Jerusalem. En route, the group sang a hymn (Matthew 26:30). And as they walked, Jesus taught them, as He had done for the three previous years. His most shocking revelation was that "the hour is coming, yes, has now come, that you will be scattered, each to his own, and will leave Me alone" (John 16:32).

Somewhere between the Upper Room and the Garden of Gethsemane the Master uttered His most intimate prayer—His high priestly prayer, which is recorded in John 17. In it He interceded for His disciples and for all who would trust in Him as Saviour. Just where He prayed this prayer, the true "Lord's

**The Garden of
Gethsemane**

Prayer," is uncertain. The rugged streets of Jerusalem do not provide the proper atmosphere for such a solemn prayer. Perhaps He stopped for one last time in the temple courts. When He had cleansed it the last time and had made it suitable for such a prayer as this, He said, "My house shall be called a house of prayer" (Matthew 21:13).

Finally, Christ and the disciples crossed the Kidron and arrived at the Garden of Gethsemane (John 18:1). There He left the disciples, taking Peter, James and John deeper into the night shadows. There, too, He left these three, the inner circle, and went a stone's throw farther to pray (Luke 22:41). Three times He returned from private prayer to find the disciples sleeping (Mark 14:39-41).

Then it happened. Suddenly a multitude appeared, piercing the quiet of the chilly night. Judas led the mob, which included the chief priests, scribes and elders. With the words, "Master, Master," and a kiss of betrayal, Judas' treachery was over (Mark 14:43-50). Brandishing swords and staves, they apprehended the Saviour and led Him away.

THURSDAY, MIDNIGHT. Only the Gospel of John records that Jesus was first led to the HOUSE OF ANNAS. It was here that Jesus was questioned concerning His doctrine and was cruelly struck by one of the officers of Annas (John 18:13-23).

From there, Jesus was led to the HOUSE OF CAIAPHAS, the high priest (Mark 14:53-72). The assembled Sanhedrin made a miserable and unsuccessful attempt to frame Jesus with the testimony of false witnesses. But the buffoons who were testifying against Jesus could not get their stories to agree, and the frame failed. In desperation Caiaphas asked Jesus point-blank, "Are you the Christ?" With crisp directness Jesus answered, "I am" (Mark 14:53-65). Caiaphas decided he had Him. Jesus would be charged with blasphemy. So ended His first trial.

FRIDAY, A.M. During the predawn hours the scene changed. The Sanhedrin reconvened; and after they had found Christ guilty of blasphemy, they sent Him to the residence of Pilate. It is just a short walk from the southeast sector of the city to the palace-garrison where it is believed Pilate lodged when he was in Jerusalem. This was the FORTRESS OF ANTONIO.

Located at the northwest corner of the temple compound, this castle was built by Herod the Great in 36 B.C. and named in honor of his friend, Marc Anthony. This huge quadrangle with massive towers at each corner was really a city within a city. A Roman legion was stationed there to guard against any trouble that might be sparked in the temple area. When Paul was seized by the Jews in the temple, the chief captain took soldiers and centurions from the Fortress of Antonio to rescue him from the Jewish mob (Acts 21:30-40).

Saint Peter in Gallicantu Church

THE HOUSE OF CAIAPHAS

There are two rivals for the site of Caiaphas' House. The first is located just north of the Dormition Abbey toward the Zion Gate. The ruins of this arched church are under the care of the Armenian Church. Nearby you can see the carved marble tombs of fifteenth-century Armenian patriarchs.

The other site is the SAINT PETER IN GALLICANTU CHURCH. This is south of the Dung Gate and on the eastern slope of a hill overlooking the Kidron and Hinnom Valleys, above the Pool of Siloam. The Assumptionist Fathers built this church in 1931. It is a quaint-looking building with a colorful mosaic facade. Entrance is through a narrow doorway on the upper side of the church.

From the foyer you can see the main sanctuary, beautifully decorated around the ceiling and equipped with hard benches. Here one of the Assumptionist Fathers will tell you the story of Jesus' first trial. A stairway leads from the foyer to a chapel below. If you go down yet another set of steps, you can enter the dungeon. This is likely the guardroom where Jesus was kept prisoner by the high priest Caiaphas.

As you ascend to leave this lovely church, don't miss the view from the balcony. From there you can see the Kidron Valley, the Hinnom Valley and the Field of Haceldama.

You may be asking yourself about the name of the church, Saint Peter in Gallicantu. "Gallicantu" means "cockcrow" and the church is consecrated to commemorate Peter's triple denial of Jesus (Luke 22:54-62) and his remorse after he heard the cock crow. The church is built over the remains of a Byzantine monastery and grotto where the apostle is said to have wept over his unfaithfulness. Mark attests that "Peter was below in the courtyard," denied the Lord three times, "and when he thought about it, he wept" (Mark 14:66,72).

At this site, archaeologists have discovered an ancient stone mill, houses, baths, an almost complete set of Hebrew measures and the remains of Hasmonean steps leading from the hill down to Siloam. It may have been that, while these were being used, Jesus was being accused falsely and convicted unjustly by desperate men on a desolate night.

When Pilate received Jesus, he immediately asked, "Are You the King of the Jews?" Jesus' affirmative response provoked Pilate to admit, "I find no fault in this Man." But further accusations by the now fiercely bitter chief priests stirred up the Jews and provided Pilate with the perfect excuse for inaction. When he learned that Jesus was a Galilean and therefore under the jurisdiction of Herod Antipas (who was in Jerusalem at the time), Pilate quickly sent our Lord to the king (Luke 23:1-7).

If the Jerusalem palace was the scene where Herod received Jesus, the route that the Lord had taken to get there was across the Old City. The traditional site of HEROD'S PALACE is adjacent to the Citadel. This site where Jesus and Herod met face to face, across the moat from the Citadel's southeast tower, is now the site of a Jerusalem police barracks.

Herod, whom Jesus had previously called "that fox" (Luke 13:32), was in Jerusalem at that time for the festivities of the Passover. He was undoubtedly more anxious to meet the Messiah than Jesus was to meet him. Luke records, "Now when Herod saw Jesus, he was exceedingly glad; for he had desired for a long time to see Him, because he had heard many things about Him, and he hoped to see some miracle done by Him" (Luke 23:8). But there would be no miracles today. In fact, when the chief priests and scribes vehemently accused Jesus, He wouldn't even respond. Frustrated, Herod "mocked Him, arrayed Him in a gorgeous robe, and sent Him back to Pilate" (Luke 23:11).

A return to Pilate meant a return to the Antonio Fortress. Caught between his superstitious fears and the strident demands of the Jews, Pilate proposed a solution that he hoped would satisfy those who were calling for Jesus' blood. Christ would be scourged, flogged with leather whips that were tipped with pieces of metal or bone to increase the pain. Surely that would satisfy the Jews. It didn't (Luke 23:13-26).

Pilate's next ploy was to remind the Jews that it was the governor's custom at the feast to release a prisoner, a custom designed to secure the favor of the people. Mark notes that Pilate asked the crowd, "Do you want me to release to you the King of the Jews? . . . But the chief priests stirred up the crowd, so that he should rather release Barabbas to them" (Mark 15:9,11). Pilate's attempt to sidestep the problem of Jesus had failed again.

Street near the Via Dolorosa

To Pilate's query about what to do with Jesus, the corridors of time still ring with the chilling cry, "Crucify him!" But Pilate's wife revealed a dream to her husband, warning him not to involve himself with this innocent man. Pilate had only one more option, one last opportunity to disengage himself from this politically volatile situation.

Mark writes, "Then the soldiers led Him away into the hall called Praetorium, and they called together the whole garrison. And they clothed Him with purple; and they twisted a crown of thorns, put it on His head, and began to salute Him, 'Hail, King of the Jews!' Then they struck Him on the head with a reed and spat on Him; and bowing the knee, they worshiped Him" (Mark 15:16-19).

FRIDAY, 6:00 A.M. This cruelty completed, Pilate again appeared with Jesus before the crowds. Declaring insistently that he still found no fault in Him, Pilate displayed the Lord wearing the purple robe and crown of thorns. His declaration, "Behold the Man!" (John 19:5) must be understood as "See what I've done to this innocent man. What more do you want?" The response was swift and decisive. "When the chief priests and officers saw Him, they cried out, saying, 'Crucify Him, crucify Him!'" (John 19:6). The die was cast.

It is possible to visit these sites today.

From Lion's Gate, walk into the Old City along the VIA DOLOROSA, which means the "Way of Sorrow." This street, the most famous street in Christendom, became the way of the cross. Since the first century millions of pilgrims have made the trek over the stones of this sacred street. The Via Dolorosa and the Church of the Holy Sepulchre exhibit the 14 STATIONS OF THE CROSS. Every Friday at 3:00 p.m. a procession, led by Franciscan priests, is conducted along this route. Indulgences are awarded to Catholics who make this pilgrimage.

Many of these 14 stations are based solely on tradition, and the events that they commemorate are missing from the pages of the Gospels. Nonetheless, let's trace the traditional steps from Pilate's Judgment Hall to Calvary.

STATION ONE. *Jesus was condemned to death.*
The present Saint Mary's Street, which begins at the Lion's Gate and continues as the Via Dolorosa, runs directly through the center of what used to be the Antonio Fortress. Hence, the first station of the cross is to your left after you pass the Church of Saint Anne. Here Jesus was mocked, crowned with thorns and condemned. This was the Praetorium, Pilate's Judgment Hall (Mark 15:16).

The site today, which is above the ruins of the Antonio, is a Muslim boys' school known as El Omariye. A staircase known as the Scala Santa (The Holy Steps), reported to be where Pilate stood as he washed his hands of Jesus' case, were removed to Rome by Constantine's mother, Helena. The remains can be seen in the Scala Santa Church near St. John in the Lateran. On the upper level of the El Omariye courtyard is a small domed Crusader chapel known as the CHAPEL OF THE CROWNING OF THE THORNS. This commemorates one of history's most dreadful acts.

STATION TWO. *Jesus received the cross.*
Two important chapels of a Franciscan monastery are on the opposite side of the Antonio Fortress, across the street from the Praetorium. On the wall outside the entrance to the monastery is a small plaque indicating "II Statio" (Station Two). Within the Franciscan compound is the CHAPEL OF THE FLAGELLATION. It stands on the traditional site of Jesus' scourging.

This medieval structure is beautifully decorated in the Crusader style and contains three stained-glass windows by Cambellotti. The windows depict the flagellation, Pilate washing his hands and Barabbas' release. A crown of thorns hangs over the sanctuary. There is also an altar to Saint Paul as he, too, was imprisoned in the Antonio (Acts 21—23).

The other chapel in the compound is the CHAPEL OF CONDEMNATION, and it marks the site where Pilate sentenced Jesus. The square Byzantine building features a dome, the windows of which depict angels with instruments of torture. Here you can see ancient

flagstones which made up the pavement floor of the Antonio. The largest portion of this floor is visible in the convent next door.

The CONVENT OF THE SISTERS OF ZION, located just a few yards deeper into the Old City on the Via Dolorosa, was founded by a Christian Jew, Father Alphonse Ratisbone, of Strasbourg, France. When you enter the convent, you will gather with others in the room to your right for an informative lecture on the events that took place here that eventful night.

Then you go downstairs to the chapel. The wall above and behind the altar is of special interest. Look to the right corner of the altar. There you can plainly see the outline of an arch. This arch continues through the wall of the chapel and out over the Via Dolorosa until it is attached to the buildings on the opposite side of the street. This is the famous ECCE HOMO ARCH.

This arch is named "Ecce Homo" ("Behold the Man") because it is believed that here Pilate presented Jesus to the crowd after He was flogged, dressed in a robe and crowned with thorns (John 19:5). Actually the arch has nothing to do with this event. The arch was built by Hadrian in A.D. 135 and was part of the emperor's triple triumphal gate into Aelia Capitolina. Nonetheless, the sight of the arch continues to inspire those who walk the Via Dolorosa because of the event that took place there.

From this chapel, go down a flight of stairs to the ground level of Jesus' day. There, in an arched room with an exceptionally low

**Roman pavement under the
Convent of the Sisters of Zion**

ceiling, you reach the pavement of the Antonio Fortress. This was the original Via Dolorosa. John 19:13 records, "When Pilate therefore heard that saying, he brought Jesus out and sat down in the judgment seat in a place that is called The Pavement, but in Hebrew, Gabbatha."

Some Christians believe this is the site of the Praetorium, rather than the area across the street. Others hold that Pilate's private meeting with Jesus was held there while he judged our Lord publicly here.

Known as the LITHOSTROTOS in Greek, the flagstones of this large paved square within the Antonio Fortress covered about a third of the western section of the palace. Notice the way the stones are striated. In fact, put your hand on them and feel them. Many of the flagstones have ridges, or grooves, in them, designed to prevent horses from losing their footing. A bit farther along are some stones with circles and squares marked on them. These etchings were made by the Roman soldiers for use in games that helped them while away the hours of duty.

The king's game—etchings in the pavement made by Roman soldiers

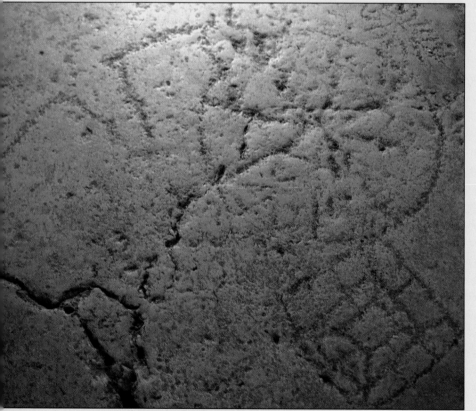

Underneath the Lithostrotos were enormous double rock-hewn cisterns. Some of the ridges of the flagstones acted as channels for the water to flow into the cisterns. The subterranean cisterns may be visited, but you can also see them through iron grates as you leave the Lithostrotos to ascend to street level. The stairs bring you to the Sisters of Zion bookstore, where fascinating volumes pertaining to the life of our Lord and these sacred sites are sold. Other souvenirs are available as well.

STATION THREE. *Jesus fell the first time.*

At the point where the Via Dolorosa joins El-Wad Road and bends sharply to the left, you will see a small Polish chapel. The relief over the door shows Jesus fallen beneath the load of His cross. Attached to the chapel is the Polish Roman Catholic Biblical-Archaeological Museum. This site marks the third station of the cross. However, the event is not recorded in the Bible.

STATION FOUR. *Jesus met Mary His mother.*

An Armenian Catholic church named OUR LADY OF THE SPASM identifies Station Four. About 75 feet from the corner at Station Three and on the same (left) side of the street, this station is marked by a beautiful relief over the door. Jesus, bearing cross and crown, is shown being comforted by His mother. This is the most attractive marker for a station of the cross. The church is believed to stand on the site of the Byzantine Church of Saint Sophia. In the church's sixth-century crypt, a mosaic shows the footprints that are supposed to have been those left by Mary when she met the Christ.

STATION FIVE. *Simon compelled to carry Jesus' cross.*

Mark 15:21 tells us that after releasing Jesus to the mob, "they compelled a certain man, Simon a Cyrenian, the father of Alexander and Rufus, as he was coming out of the country and passing by, to bear His cross." Station Five marks this event. A small depression in the stone face of the nine-teenth-century Franciscan chapel that commemorates this occasion is said to be the place where Jesus rested His hand under the weight of the cross (Matthew 27:32; Luke 23:26). Simon was a native of Libya, North Africa, and was in Jerusalem for the Passover. His sons were closely associated with the Christian church.

STATION SIX. *Veronica wiped Jesus' face.*

A Greek Orthodox Catholic chapel served by the Little Sisters stands on the left of the Via Dolorosa, about halfway between the two streets that angle away from each other at the Damascus Gate. This is the traditional site where a woman named Veronica wiped the blood and sweat from Jesus' marred face. According to legend, when Veronica looked at the cloth, she found the imprint of Christ's face had remained. This probably accounts for the woman's name ("vera icone" meaning "true image"). Supposedly, Veronica was the woman cured simply by touching the hem of Jesus' garment. However, the woman's very existence, as well as her act of kindness, is based on tradition alone.

STATION SEVEN. *Jesus fell the second time.*

Station Seven is located near the corner of the Via Dolorosa and Suq Khan Ez-Zeit (which leads directly to the Damascus Gate). Adjacent to the market wall upon which this station is marked are two Franciscan chapels. In one of them there is a reddish stone column thought to be a marker for the crossroads of main streets in Hadrian's city, Aelia Capitolina.

STATION EIGHT. *Jesus conversed with some women of Jerusalem.*

Luke records that a great number of women followed Jesus as He was led to Calvary. The women "mourned and lamented Him." The Lord stopped, turned toward them and said, "Daughters of Jerusalem, do not weep for Me, but weep for yourselves and for your children" (Luke 23:27,28). He then prophe-sied the weeping and wailing that would accompany the coming destruction of Jerusalem. Station Eight commemorates this occasion. This station on El-Khanqa Street is marked by a cross engraved in a circle on a wall of the GREEK ORTHODOX MONASTERY OF SAINT CHARALAMBOS.

STATION NINE. *Jesus fell the third time.*

At the entrance to a Coptic monastery, located on an alley leading west from Suq Khan Ez-Zeit, there is a round Roman column. Tradition claims that at this spot Jesus fell the third time. (None of these falls is recorded in

Interior of the Church of the Holy Sepulchre

THE CHURCH OF THE HOLY SEPULCHRE

When Hadrian ruled the city as Aelia Capitolina, he covered the site of the Church of the Holy Sepulchre (and most of Jerusalem) with pagan shrines and temples. It was not until Queen Helena, mother of Constantine, came here that this site traditionally became identified with Calvary. Constantine built the original church in 326. This church was destroyed by the Persians in 614. Just two years later, Abbot Modestos, the Greek Orthodox Patriarch, rebuilt the edifice, only to have it razed by the mad Egyptian Khalif Al-Hakim in 1010. The Crusaders again rebuilt the church; but when they were defeated by Saladin in 1187, the Christian community was permitted to use the church only if the keys to the church remained in Muslim hands. Since 1330, the right of entry to Christianity's most noted church has remained in the hands of the Arab Nuseibeh family.

Today the church is a conglomeration. Every few feet the decor changes because every few feet the jurisdiction changes. There is no theme, no architectural plan, no predominant period. Byzantine, Crusader and nineteenth-century Greek styles are in evidence, covering 1500 years of construction.

Fires, earthquakes and the ravages of the centuries have left the church in a deplorable state. Between 1936 and 1944, the British installed ugly steel reinforcements to prevent the church from collapsing. In 1958, a program of "total restoration" was proposed but in-fighting among the religious orders has not made restoration "total." At best, it's an ongoing task.

Scripture.) The Coptic Church itself is interesting, for within its whitewashed walls Abyssinian monks live and serve. Beneath the edifice is an immense cistern.

Stations 10 through 14 are located within the walls of Christendom's most prominent church—Jerusalem's CHURCH OF THE HOLY SEPULCHRE. Those orders that have major jurisdiction over the church are the Roman Catholic, Greek Catholic and Armenian Orthodox Catholic. Minor jurisdiction is claimed by the Syrian (Jacobite) Catholic, Coptic Catholic and Abyssinian Catholic orders.

The two-story church, with its twelfth-century Romanesque facade, is entered through double portals with pointed arches. You enter through the left portal, since the other door was walled up in Saladin's day. Directly ahead is a polished red slab known as the STONE OF UNCTION, the traditional site where Jesus' body was anointed for burial. To the left is the great rotunda of the church. The steps to the right, just before the stone, lead to the Latin and Greek chapels that contain Stations 10 through 13. According to Catholic tradition, these second-story chapels are built over Mount Calvary.

STATION TEN. *Jesus stripped of His garments.*

We ascend the stairs to the Franciscan chapel, the southern nave. This station is commemorated by a mosaic representation on the floor, the pattern of which depicts Abraham sacrificing Isaac, which is symbolic of Christ's sacrifice. According to tradition, this is where Jesus was stripped of His garments and was given gall to drink (Mark 15:23,24; Luke 23:34).

STATION ELEVEN. *Jesus nailed to the cross.*

In the southeast corner of the Franciscan chapel you will find Station 11. It is marked by the main altar, the Medici Altar. Behind the altar on the wall is a mosaic scene depicting the nailing of Christ to Calvary's cross (Matthew 27:35; John 19:18).

STATION TWELVE. *Jesus was crucified and died on the cross.*

The main altar is in the north nave, in the Greek side of the chapel, in the northeast corner. This marks the traditional site of the crucifixion and death of our Lord (Mark 15:25, 37; Luke 23:46). Under the altar a silver star/disc

indicates where Christ's cross was dropped into the ground. Two black discs, one on each side of the altar, mark where the thieves' crosses were planted. A fissure in the rock, on the right side of the altar, is reported to have been created by the earthquake that accompanied Jesus' crucifixion.

STATION THIRTEEN. *Jesus' body removed from the cross.*

Between Station 11 and Station 12 you will see an antique wooden bust of Mary, mother of Jesus. This marks Station 13. The bust is in a glass case which belongs to the Franciscans and is laden with jewels and gold, votive offerings from Catholic pilgrims through the centuries. The actual site of the removal of Christ from the cross, according to Catholic tradition, is under the Franciscan altar.

There are many other chapels in this church. For example, down the stairs at the extreme eastern end of the church you can visit the CHURCH OF SAINT HELENA. The main altar, at the far end, is dedicated to Helena, who first identified most of the sacred sites in the

Catholic tradition. To the right of the altar a stairway leads down to the CHAPEL OF THE DISCOVERY OF THE CROSS. According to tradition, this place was once a cistern at the foot of Calvary into which the three crosses were tossed. Helena directed the search and found the "true cross" of Christ. It is evident, however, that most of the chapels within the Church of the Holy Sepulchre are based on one tradition or another. Many visitors, Catholic and Protestant alike, quickly tire of peering into chapel after chapel.

To reach the last station, you must descend the stairs to the main level of the church. On the way to that station, you will pass the KATHOLIKON, the open center of the church, which is actually a Greek cathedral. Here a stone chalice, centered on the Crusader floor of the cathedral, is reported to mark THE CENTER OF THE EARTH. This medieval tradition arose because the site is midway between the traditional Calvary and the sepulcher.

Just west of here you enter the ROTUNDA. This area is under a massive nineteenth-century dome, 65 feet in diameter. It is enclosed

IS THE CHURCH OF THE HOLY SEPULCHRE THE SITE OF CALVARY?

For centuries, doubts have been raised about the authenticity of the Church of the Holy Sepulchre as the site of the crucifixion. Periodically, people have asked whether or not the church was really outside the first-century wall. Bits of information have led some to place Calvary at other locations. One early author from Bordeaux, France, wrote in A.D. 333:

"As you leave there and pass through the wall of Zion towards the gate of Neapolis [Nablus or Damascus Gate] . . . on your left is the hillock Golgotha where the Lord was crucified, and about

a stone's throw from it to the vault where they laid his body and he rose again on the third day."

The site near the Garden Tomb fits this description.

In 1883, General Charles Gordon became convinced that this was indeed the Place of the Skull. Gordon died a hero at Khartoum in the Sudan a short time later, and this Skull Hill site became popularly known as GORDON'S CALVARY. Most Protestants accept Gordon's identification as a possible alternative to the Church of the Holy Sepulchre.

by a circular corridor that is formed by 18 gigantic columns that support the dome. The upper galleries of the Rotunda are divided into many chapels and chambers that belong to the three major religious communities that share the church. The final station involving the cross is at the center of the Rotunda.

STATION FOURTEEN. *Jesus buried in a sepulcher.*

The traditional tomb of Jesus is enclosed in a tiny, richly ornamented nineteenth-century building which serves as a shrine. It is free-standing and positioned in the middle of the church. The decor is so extravagant that it detracts from the site it commemorates. The box-like structure is crowned with a cupola of the Muscovite style. It is approached through a small chamber, or vestibule, known as the CHAPEL OF THE ANGEL. Supposedly the angel sat here on the stone and announced the Lord's resurrection (Mark 16:5-7). A pedestal in the center displays what is said to be bits of the actual stone used to seal Jesus' tomb. Three separate pictures of the resurrection hang over the entrance—one belonging to the Latins, one to the Greeks and one to the Armenians.

The entrance to the tomb itself is low and very narrow. Not all Christian pilgrims find it easy to get through it. The inside of the chamber is miniscule, six and one-half feet long and six feet wide. Only four or five people can fit into the tomb-chamber at a time. All around are religious artifacts and tiny lamps. To the right is a white marble slab that covers the burial niche. The stone beneath it is said to be the burial place of Jesus.

As you make your way back through the church, you will mingle with tourists from all nations and all religions. You'll rub elbows with monks and nuns from various orders, attired in various-colored robes. The church is overly ornate and confusing, and you won't get a sense of being at the tomb at all. Nevertheless, there is a certain excitement that attends your visit. If you are really looking for excitement, visit the church during the festivities of Easter week. You'll need a program to follow all the activity.

To a large extent, the Stations of the Cross are based on tradition. So, let's reconstruct the events of that last day in light of Scripture.

FRIDAY, 9:00 A.M. Upon release by Pilate, Jesus was driven by the crowds to "a place called Golgotha, that is to say, Place of a Skull" (Matthew 27:33; Mark 15:22). Luke calls this crucifixion site by its Latin name, Calvary. Here Jesus was crucified in full view of the passersby. Here He died on the cross.

Although the exact location of the crucifixion has been disputed over the years, we do know that it was outside Jerusalem. The writer of Hebrews said, "Therefore Jesus also, that He might sanctify the people with His own blood, suffered outside the gate" (Hebrews 13:12). Pilate placed a title on Jesus' cross: "JESUS OF NAZARETH, THE KING OF THE JEWS." John explains, "Then many of the Jews read this title, for the place where Jesus was crucified was near the city" (John 19:20). So while Jesus' cross was placed outside the gate of the city, it was nevertheless not far from that gate and where many travelers could see the shame of the cross.

You don't have to go far from the Damascus Gate to see such a site today.

Walk up Salah ed Din Street, less than a block from the famous gate, and on your right you will see a stone wall through which an alley leads to a beautiful and restful compound. This is the GARDEN TOMB. There are no altars, no orders and no chapels here.

The tomb near Golgotha

Rather, you'll find trees, birds and flowers.

Enter through a bookstore foyer. When you step down into the garden, you may be invited to take a seat on a bench to listen to the warden of the garden explain the history and importance of the site. To the right is a long but pleasant path that leads to a platform at the far southeastern edge of the garden. From the top of the platform you have a grand view of what is thought to be THE PLACE OF THE SKULL.

As you stare at the scarp of rock—a line of cliffs produced by faulting or erosion—you can clearly see what looks like the deep-set sockets of skull eyes. Try to erase from your mind the Muslim cemetery on top of the hill and the noisy bus station below. Critics of the site say that the eye sockets were cisterns broken out when quarrying was done in the area after the time of Christ. Advocates say that this quarrying was part of the operation that took place when stone was taken to build Solomon's Temple (I Kings 5:15; 6:7). Just north of the Damascus Gate you can look through an iron gate and see a cavernous quarry through a seven-foot fissure in the bedrock of Jerusalem.

If the advocates are correct, the face of the skull would have been present in Jesus' day. And if so, we are viewing CALVARY, the place of crucifixion, the Place of the Skull. On this hill, or perhaps on the level area in front of it, Jesus Christ bled and died to atone for man's sin.

FRIDAY, NOON. From the time He was lifted up on the cross (John 3:14-18) at about 9:00 a.m. until noon the Lord spoke just three times. He prayed for the Father to forgive His tormentors (Luke 23:34; Isaiah 53:12); He forgave the thief and gave him assurance (Luke 23:43); and He spoke to His mother and to John (John 19:26,27).

Then suddenly it happened. Each of the Synoptic Gospels records the strange phenomenon. From noon until 3:00 p.m. an inky darkness filled the land (Matthew 27:45, 51-53).

FRIDAY, 3:00 P.M. The silence is broken as light returns. The Saviour cries to God in the language of Psalm 22 (Matthew 27:46); quietly He refers to His thirst (John 19:28; Psalm 69:21); victoriously He shouts, "It is finished" (John 19:30); finally He commends His life unto God (Luke 23:46). Jesus is dead.

Don't leave this platform too quickly. Meditate on the hill before you. Knowing the site of the Saviour's crucifixion is not as important as knowing the Saviour Himself. God has always demanded a blood sacrifice in payment for sin. He demanded it of Adam (Genesis 3:6,7,21). He demanded it of Cain (Genesis 4:3-5). He demanded it of the Israelites (Exodus 12:12,13). But for us, He demanded it of Christ. "God demonstrates His own love toward us, in that while we were still sinners, Christ died for us" (Romans 5:8). Speaking of Jesus, the Apostle Peter said it this way, "Who Himself bore our sins in His own body on the tree, that we, having died to sins, might live for righteousness" (I Peter 2:24).

There is a green hill far away,
Without a city wall,
Where our dear Lord was crucified,
Who died to save us all.
—Cecil F. Alexander

FRIDAY, 5:00 P.M. The tomb of Jesus receives only a cursory description in the Gospels. John records that Joseph of Arimathea, a secret disciple of the Lord, was joined by Nicodemus, and "then they took the body of Jesus, and bound it in strips of linen with the spices, as the custom of the Jews is to bury. Now in the place where He was crucified there was a garden, and in the garden a new tomb in which no one had yet been laid. So there they laid Jesus, because of the Jews' Preparation Day, for the tomb was nearby" (John 19:40-42).

Let's steal away now, down the path and through the garden. The fact that this is a restful spot now, the type you would expect to find Jesus buried in, doesn't necessarily mean it was a garden in the first century. But the ancient wine or oil press located along

The Garden Tomb

IS THE GARDEN TOMB
THE TOMB OF JESUS?

The Garden Tomb winepress

The tomb of Jesus was in a garden. It was near the place of crucifixion. It was a new sepulcher, never used. Luke adds that the tomb was "hewn out of the rock" (Luke 23:53). He also notes that Jesus had to be placed in the sepulcher hurriedly because the Sabbath was approaching (Luke 23:54). If Gordon's Calvary is the place of the crucifixion, perhaps this is the tomb of Jesus. The authenticity of one is not dependent upon the authenticity of the other. But the association can hardly be coincidental.

Critics of the Garden Tomb have identified it as a third- or fourth-century tomb. Others have said it may be Byzantine. Still, one noted and respected archaeologist, Dame Kathleen Kenyon, affirms that it is typical of a first-century Jewish tomb. The debate will continue.

the path proves that this indeed was an ancient orchard. Near the upper path there is also a huge cistern, one of the largest in Jerusalem, with a capacity of nearly 238,000 gallons. This cistern indicates that the site was a garden.

At the north end of the garden is a partially-submerged tomb hewn out of the scarp. The tomb and the lovely garden in which it is located are meticulously maintained by the Garden Tomb Association of London. There is perhaps no more peaceful setting in all of Jerusalem than the Garden Tomb. Here you can quietly meditate on the Lord's death, burial and resurrection.

The smallish opening of the tomb (five feet high, two feet four inches wide) is a little above the sepulcher floor. You must step down to enter. It is obvious that this was no simple tomb, no peasant's sepulcher. There are two distinct chambers in the tomb. The first is ten feet long and eight feet wide. There is a grave trough at the back, or the northern, end. To your right is a doorway with a barred gate. Through this doorway is an eastern chamber. There, against the back wall, is a near perfect burial site. The back and ends are formed by the rock-hewn walls of the tomb. The front slab of the site is missing, but a "sitting" stone is visible on both ends (John 20:11,12). The rock is a brownish color and its chisel marks show that it has been carved out of the rock.

You are looking at what may be THE tomb of Jesus. It forces you to stop and think. The remarkable thing about the tomb is not its craftsmanship, not its remarkable state of preservation, not even its quiet restfulness. The remarkable thing about the tomb is that it's empty. "But the angel answered and said to the women, 'Do not be afraid, for I know that you seek Jesus who was crucified. He is not here; for He is risen, as He said. Come, see the place where the Lord lay'" (Matthew 28:5,6). This is what makes a journey to the Holy Land "holy"—the personal discovery that HE IS NOT HERE; FOR HE IS RISEN.

For more than half a century, millions of people throughout the world have been challenged, directed and comforted through the ministry of Back to the Bible.

Now, under the leadership of Dr. Woodrow Kroll, the ministry continues its outreach by radio, literature, counseling and missions, through a worldwide network of nine international offices.

Helping people understand that the Bible is practical and relevant to life in the '90s is the primary focus of Dr. Kroll's ministry. As Bible teacher on the daily radio broadcast, heard on more than 600 stations worldwide, and as producer of PASSPORT VIDEO, Woodrow Kroll evidences a life of dedication to teaching the Word of God.

Lincoln, Nebraska, is the international headquarters of Back to the Bible. For questions about the ministry or *Bible Country* please write to Back to the Bible, Box 82808, Lincoln, Nebraska 68501.

INDEX

Photo Credits

V. Gilbert Beers
> 6 (left), 6 (top center), 6 (bottom center), 7 (top right), 16, 19 (above), 20, 22, 26, 28 (below), 33 (below), 34, 44 & 45, 45, 48, 50, 51, 52 (below), 54, 56 & 57, 60, 62, 65, 66 (left), 70, 72 (above), 72 (below), 74 & 75, 76, 77, 81, 82, 85, 87 (above), 89 (above), 89 (below), 92 (above), 92 (below), 93, 99 (left), 100, 104, 109 (below), 110, 116, 118 (above), 119, 120 (left), 120 (right), 121, 124, 125, 126, 129 (above), 129 (below), 130, 131, 132 (above), 132 (below), 133, 134, 140 (above), 140 (below), 148 (above), 154 (above), 154 (below), 166, 171

Paul Blasco
> 18 (below), 31, 35 (above), 35 (below), 138 (below), 148 (below)

Holy Views, Ltd.
> 63 (below), 77 (above), 79, 97 (above), 175

Israel Colour Slides
> 55 (below)

Dr. Jim Jennings
> 84, 98

Jerusalem Photographers Co., Ltd.
> 63 (above), 101 (below)

Tom Kilpatrick
> 8, 10, 11, 12, 30, 33 (above), 74 (left), 152, 157, 159 (below), 160, 162

Woodrow Kroll
> 5, 6 & 7, 7 (center), 7 (bottom right), 9, 13, 14, 18 (above), 32, 36, 37, 38, 40, 46, 49 (above), 49 (below), 53, 55 (above), 58, 59 (above), 59 (below), 61, 66 (right), 67, 68, 75 (below), 80, 88 (below), 90, 94 (left), 99 (right), 103, 105, 108 (below), 109 (above), 113, 114 (above), 114 (below), 118 (below), 122, 123 (above), 127, 128, 134 (above), 134 (below), 142, 146, 147 (above), 149, 153 (above), 153 (below), 155, 158 (below), 164, 165, 168, 169, 170 (left), 170 (right), 172, 173, 174, 177, 178, 179, 181, 182

Loretta C. Nelson
> 19 (below), 21, 28 (above), 42, 47, 52 (above), 61 (above), 69, 86, 87 (below), 88 (above), 91, 94 (right), 95, 97 (below), 101 (above), 102, 106, 111, 112, 123 (below), 135, 136, 138 (above), 139, 141 (above), 141 (below), 147 (below), 150 & 151, 151, 156, 158 (above), 159 (above), 163

Palestine Archeological Museum
> 96

Tom Schindler
> 144

Photographer unknown
> 78, 108 (above)

Back to the Bible is a nonprofit ministry dedicated to Bible teaching, evangelism and edification of Christians worldwide.

If we may assist you in knowing more about Christ and the Christian life, please write to us without obligation.

Back to the Bible
P.O. Box 82808
Lincoln, NE 68501